SERVICE MARKETING

SERVICE MARKETING

Dr. K. Sravana
Dr. Manita Matharu
Dr. Manish Joshi
Dr. P. Jagadeesan
Dr. P. Balaji

SERVICE MARKETING

by: Dr. K. Sravana, Dr. Manita Matharu, Dr. Manish Joshi, Dr. P. Jagadeesan, Dr. P. Balaji

■

RED'SHINE PUBLICATION PVT. LTD.

Headquarters (India): 88-90 REDMAC, Navamuvada,
Lunawada, India-389 230
Contact: +91 76988 26988
Registration no. GJ31D0000034

In Association with,

RED'MAC INTERNATIONAL PRESS & MEDIA. INC

India | Sweden | UK

■

■

ISBN: 978-93-93239-53-2
ISBN-10: 9-39-323953-3
DIP: 18.10.9393239533
DOI: 10.25215/9393239533
Price: ₹ 400
December, 2021 (First Edition)

■

■

www.redshine.co.in | info@redshine.in
Printed in India | Title ID: 9393239533

PREFACE

The world economy nowadays is increasingly characterized as a service economy. This is primarily due to the increasing importance and share of the service sector in the economies of most developed and developing countries. In fact, the growth of the service sector has long been considered as indicative of a country's economic progress. Economic history tells us that all developing nations have invariably experienced a shift from agriculture to industry and then to the service sector as the main stay of the economy.

This is an academic book which covering all the basic concepts of service marketing and recent trends also. So that students of undergraduate and post graduate level can easily follow as the lay out of the contents are simple and understandable.

Authors

CONTENTS

MODULE – 1

INTRODUCTION TO SERVICE MARKETING

A large portion of the enterprise market is made up of services. The service area has grown significantly. It is the most populous region in the majority of economies, and it is also the fastest-growing in a big number of those. By definition, advanced economies are basically issuer economies, where the service sector is responsible for the vast majority of employment and financial gain. Services contribute far too much to GDP and employment, especially in advanced economies.

Although the percentage of offerings inside the GDP of developing economies is decrease than within the advanced ones, the company place has been growing very speedy within the developing global. During 1980-1990 the common annual increase charge of fee brought inside the provider vicinity in the developing economies became 3.5 in keeping with cent compared to the GDP increase price of three consistent with cent.

The issuer quarter of India grew at 6.9 in keeping with cent and seven nine consistent with cent throughout the above intervals, in assessment to the corresponding GDP increase quotes of 5. Eight in keeping with cent and five. Nine in step with cent. The percent of offerings within the GDP of India increased from 36 in keeping with cent to 48 percentages in 2001.

It is not clean to estimate the proportion of the financial offerings in the offerings quarter. It is, but, not unusual understanding that it's miles pretty massive. The commercial offerings market has been developing very speedy.

Some of the substantial improvement which contributed to the expansion of the offerings market is the subsequent.

As Berry observes, even as a product is an item, devise or physical thing, a service is a deed, usual overall performance, or effort. "As with merchandise, each commercial enterprise service represents a bundle of need pleasing attributes. These attributes are supplied to a consumer thru the service experience. The time period revel in is used to connote all additives of individual-to-man or woman customer service interaction. In offering a selected want-exciting experience to a client, the marketer is said to be 'turning in' a issuer'."

Pyne defines provider as – "a hobby which has a few detail of intangibility associated with it which includes a few interplay-with customers for assets in their ownership, and does not bring about a switch possession. A change within the situation many arise and production of the issuer may additionally or might not be carefully associated with a physical product."

On the premise of the amount of provider detail worried in a organization's provide to the market vicinity, Kotler distinguishes the following five instructions of offer –

1. A natural tangible true, like screw or lubricant, and not the use of a provider accompanying the product.
2. A tangible accurate with supplementary service, like CNC lathe.
3. A hybrid, wherein the offer consists of greater or much less identical components of goods and offerings which include – eating places which can be patronize both for their meals and provider.
4. A essential provider with related moderate goods and services. For example, airline passengers are supplied with some food and drink etc., all through the air tour.
5. A natural provider, like consultancy.

WHAT IS SERVICE MARKETING – MEANING

A service is proceeds, deed, performance or a illustration presented by way of one character to some other. In a literal experience a provider does not involve the switch of any tangible commodity.

Service advertising is a method which promotes and showcases the intangible advantages and services introduced via a business enterprise to force stop purchaser cost. Sectors like hospitality, tourism, financial offerings, and expert services and so on. Use service marketing to drive their commercial enterprise.

In today's world, service is an essential component of human existence. Services have become more professional as a result of liberalisation, privatisation, and globalisation. It used to be seen of as a "social service" in the past, but with time, it has been commercialised and viewed as a business opportunity. When a corporation succeeds, it is a business interest carried out by one person to another for a fee (commercial provider).

Education, transportation, hospitality, finance and real estates are just a few examples of the wide range of services that can be provided. These services are together called the offerings region or the tertiary quarter.

We can't avoid the fact that everything grows, thus change is inevitable. From infancy until old age, a character undergoes a series of distinct transitions, each of which affects the way he perceives the world around him in various ways.

A provider is a set of consumable and perishable advantages delivered by using way of a provider residence to a client to make sure customer delight.

Goods and services are produced in each economic system. In a crude manner, a very good is something it is easy to take with him after buy, whereas a service cannot be taken as it is intangible. Example whilst a person is going to a dentist he use the offerings of the dentist and returns with a remedy. In the technique he does no longer get any physical commodity however nonetheless he has ate up a service.

Services advertising and advertising usually refers to each enterprise to customer (B2C) and industrial agency-to-enterprise (B2B) services, and consists of advertising of services which includes telecommunications offerings, financial services, all kinds of hospitality, tourism leisure and enjoyment services, car rental services, health care offerings .

For case, a cable TV company has to offer cable hookup, restore offerings and additionally excessive-definition cable boxes. Pure services, together with can be furnished by the usage of a economic consulting organisation, might also want little within the way of facilitate items, however what they do use such as textbooks, expert references, and spreadsheets are important to their performance.

DEFINITION OF SERVICE MARKETING:

Using a unique set of methods or strategies, service marketing anticipates the client's requirement for an intangible product. A difficult task is convincing customers and pricing intangible goods while selling off products.

Service marketing is advertising based on courting and value? It may be used to market a service or a product. With the increasing prominence of services in the international financial system, service marketing and advertising and marketing has come to be a subject that wants to be studied one after the opposite. Marketing services isn't always the same as marketing goods due to the precise tendencies of services specially, intangibility, and heterogeneity, perish capability and inseparability.

Service Marketing is sincerely defined as a phenomenon wherein a service or an intangible commodity is promoted and advertised a number of the target audience. A novel type of advertising, provider advertising has emerged as pretty tremendous in assisting companies promote offerings around the sector.

Service Marketing presentations at the way a type of provider is promoted inside the marketplace. Though service advertising and marketing and advertising is a completely precise concept, it calls out for an intangible representation of commodities (services).

CHARACTERISTICS OF SERVICE MARKETING

The following are the traits of services advertising:

1. Intangibility:

Services are intangible, thus they can't be touched, treated, smelt, or tasted like material products (physical senses). Due to the fact that service itself is an interest, this is the case. A company, on the other hand, can be felt. Services also instil a sense of pride in their customers. When it comes to services, there is no way to possess them because they are intangible. A service can be generated and used, but it can never be yours to begin with.

2. Perish ability:

Manufacturing a service necessitates that it be consumed at the same time. Because a provider is not a concrete item, it cannot be saved. Transport and time are both factors that affect the quality of a service. It is illegal to charge passengers for an empty seat on a plane after it has already taken off. The moment revenue leaves a location, it's gone for good.

As soon as the soliciting for provider customer receives a service, the service is gone forever because the issuer purchaser ate it up. In this example, after the passenger has arrived at the destination, he cannot be taken back there at the same time on the same day.

3. Inseparability:

Commodities can be sold at a later date, but this is not possible with services. For example, the presence of both the service provider and the person receiving the service at the same time is critical when a doctor treats a patient or a teacher instructs a student.

The issuer is crucial to the transportation of goods because he must quickly develop and deliver the service to the customer who is looking for a carrier. As a result, the company that provides the service, the carrier, and the end user are all one and the same.

4. Simultaneity:

There is a single temporal frame in which services are generated and consumed. It is imperative that the service be delivered as soon as the consumer has ordered it (delivery) without any alterations. The purchaser of the service immediately uses the supplied benefits to realise his or her aspirations. Offerings are typically made and consumed simultaneously, as a result.

5. Variability:

There is no room for error when it comes to business. There is a lack of uniformity in the services provided. An illustration of this is when a doctor sees patients with similar ailments on the same day. Patients' dignity after therapy will be completely different than it was before. The difference is due to factors such as the doctor's mood, the doctor's exhaustion level, how the issuer is viewed by the particular afflicted individual, and so on. Despite the fact that the same scientific doctor sees the same patient on different occasions, there will be a distinction in the provider.

This is due to the fact that the doctor and the patient's moods don't stay the same throughout the day. Every piece of service is unique, even if it was created by the same person. When it comes to selling specialised goods, quality control, standardisation, and the like are all factors that cannot be implemented. The services we provide are always evolving to meet the needs of our clients.

6. Ownership:

If you make a donation, you don't get anything in return. The issuer company no longer owns the service at the moment of making or delivering the service. In order to provide a service, he has the necessary physical infrastructure. Similarly, the service customer does not fully own the service at any point in time, whether during or after use. To the greatest extent, he utilizes the service.

Customers only have the experience, but the service may have been non-existent after the intake. Because an issuer is essentially an intangible product, it cannot be owned by everyone.

CLASSIFICATION OF SERVICE MARKETING

On the Basis of End User, On the Basis of Tangibility, On the Basis of Specialization and a Few Others

Services span a large number of areas in the present context. Everyday a new service is being introduced.

Though it is really difficult to classify all the services, the following classifications have been accepted:

1. On the Basis of End User:

i. **Consumer services** – Consumer services, such as hair, dressing, laundry, vacation packages, and counselling, are those that are offered directly to the end customer.

ii. **Business to business services** – This includes services such as marketing research, promotion, and consulting for firms.

2. On the Basis of Tangibility:

i. **Tangible services** For example, a television, laptop, automobile, or watch purchased from a seller may come with a limited warranty period.

ii. **Intangible services** – These are services that aren't tied to a specific product, such as a service plan or warranty. It's important to note that intangible services don't actually deliver anything tangible to the customer. Consultancy, services at a spa, and massage establishments are just a few of the examples.

3. On the Basis of Specialization:

i. **Professional services** – These are the kinds of services that can only be delivered by people who have the appropriate training and expertise these service providers may also be approved by the appropriate authorities. Counseling, auditing, legal services, health care, etc. are all examples of these services.

ii. **Nonprofessional services** – It's possible to deliver non-professional services even if you don't have any educational or professional credentials. Household services such as cleaning or gardening are among the examples.

4. On the Basis of Profit Orientation:

i. **Commercial services** – These are the services that are supplied for profit, and they are offered on business lines. Private banking, beauty salons, and the like are a few examples.

ii. **Social services** – Social services, on the other hand, are those that are provided purely for the benefit of others, with no expectation of financial reward. These services are meant to benefit the community and are hence referred to as social services. Services provided by orphanages and other philanthropic organisations are examples of this.

5. On the Basis of Labor Intensiveness:

i. **People based services** – These are services that need a significant amount of human effort. These human folks are the ones who actually supply these services. Examples include car repairs, food, event planning, and security.

ii. **Equipment based services** – This is a type of service that relies heavily on the use of specific pieces of equipment. A laborer's contribution to society is either small or non-existent. An example of this is a vending machine or an ATM that is self-activated.

6. On the Basis of Contact and Interaction between the Service Provider and the Service Consumer:

i. **High contact services** – There is a lot of back-and-forth between the service supplier and customer with these types of services. In order to perform the service, there must be some kind of touch or engagement. Mental health services include, but aren't limited to:

ii. **Low contact services** – These are the services where there is little or no interaction between the service provider and the customer. Even if there is no direct contact or engagement, the service can still be offered. Tailoring, diagnostics, and other services are examples.

SERVICE MARKETING – EXAMPLES OF SERVICES: FOOD SERVICES, HOTELS, CAR SERVICE FIRMS, ENTERTAINMENT SERVICES, TRANSPORT SERVICES AND A FEW OTHERS

1. Food Services:

There are many people and families who rely on eating out, and restaurants, cafeterias, and hotels are catering to their needs. As the public's interest for the product they sell grows, so does the number of these eating establishments. Easier and cheaper meals can be found at small restaurants.

Luxurious five-star lodges serve up sumptuous meals at opulent prices, accompanied by lavish amenities and awe-inspiring views. The growth of the resort industry has been encouraged by an increase in tourism. Aside from in-house chefs, we work with outside caterers that specialise in serving meals and hosting events in our residences for ceremonial and otherwise important occasions.

2. Hotels and Motels:

Thousands of people every day rely on lodging and lodging services. Every year, the number of hotels, resorts, and lodges grows. Travelers and tourists pay a high price to stay in modern hotels. Tourists are increasingly viewed as a major source of foreign exchange in all countries. Modern motels offer a wide range of amenities, conveniences, and services that are both modest and beautiful.

3. Personal Care Services:

The rising standard of living contributed to the development of private care services (helping a purchaser to be well groomed). Offerings include fitness and fitness centres, beauty parlours and barber shops, laundries, drycleaners, garment repair shops, shoe repair shops and so on. These services are made available through these various outlets.

Since there is an ever-growing need to enhance one's personality and productivity, health and health organisations are becoming increasingly important and popular around the world. Because of obesity, weight loss has taken on a central role in the anti-fats modern culture and way of life. There is no shortage of money, and most people are happy to spend it on themselves.

4. Car Service Firms (Garages):

There are thousands of car owners that rely on vehicle service centres (garages). As a result, gas stations have come to be referred to as "service stations." There are also a number of garages and repair shops specialising in motor vehicle repairs and renovations.

5. Entertainment Services:

There has been a steady increase in amusement offers due to an increase in shopping activity and increased time spent in amusement. There are many popular forms of organised entertainment these days, such as movies, sports, amusement parks, zoos, auto racing, cricket, pool, and stage productions such as musicals and comedies.

6. Transport Services:

There are several modes of transportation available for people and commodities to go from one place to another, including trains, buses, ships, and planes. Air delivery has seen the most rapid growth. In less than two weeks, a character will fly around the world. Air travel has become a popular mode of transportation for tourists around the world.

7. Communication Services:

The modern method to communication includes the internet, mobile, cellphone, telegraph, telex, and postal offerings that we have at our disposal today. 7. Communication Services: We also have tv, cell phone, and satellite tv for worldwide computer communications. The modern generation has been a major factor in the rapid growth of all forms of communication.

8. Insurance Services:

It's important to remember that insurance is designed to protect you from the unexpected. This includes everything from accidents to heart attacks to theft to unemployment. There are many ways to save for one's children's education, the wedding of one's daughter, or one's retirement. Insurance provides us with a sense of security and peace of mind, allowing us to live our lives without worry.

9. Financial Services:

Many clients rely on banks for financing purchases of long-lasting items, such as automobiles, through instalment payments. Even in countries where bank loans are readily available, acquiring a home is a very simple process. Loans make it possible to acquire a home with a clean conscience. Client-oriented marketing techniques by banks have made it possible for many people to live in a cutting-edge, high-end home.

IMPORTANCE OF SERVICE MARKETING

Products, services, activities, people, and so on are all types of things that can be sold by a marketer. Provider marketing is the practise of promoting and selling products and services. It is impossible to own something that is provided as a service because services are essentially immaterial. It may or may not be linked to a tangible product during the manufacturing process.

Excellence in service marketing and advertising necessitates excellence on three levels: external, internal, and interactive. Pricing, distribution and merchandising are covered by external advertising. Internal marketing encompasses educating and inspiring employees to provide excellent customer service. In interactive advertising, the ability to provide excellent customer service is described.

The importance of the offerings can be mentioned beneath the following headings:

1. **Support to Primary and Secondary Sector**- Primary sectors and secondary sectors are continuously in need of a variety of services that allow you to function easily on a normal foundation. Thus, services form a vital part for the green execution of those sectors.
2. **Creates Employment Avenues-** Service sectors create a number of employment opportunities in diverse sectors like BPOs, hospitality, retail, tourism, leisure, brokerages, software, aviation and greater. This in flip promotes and develops the general boom of the nation.
3. **Contribution to National Income-** Due to the boom and development of the service quarter, the alternative sectors inside the marketplace also are witnessing an equal increase and improvement. Moreover, because of this speedy boom and improvement of all of the sectors inside the marketplace, it mechanically contributes to the general country wide earnings of the usa.
4. **Provision for Basic Services-** Service sectors provide the u . S. With the basic offerings like hospitality, shipping, instructional institutions, courts, telecommuni-cations, insurance agencies, banks, put up offices and plenty extra. This facilitates the each day living of a commonplace man like us.
5. **Ads to Comforts and Leisure**- Service sectors offer enough comforts and enjoyment to the life of a common man. By imparting numerous offerings, it absolutely makes our lives easy and easy.
6. **Improvement in India's Image**- Various services inside the Indian marketplace like telecommunications, BPOs, software program improvement, Information Technology Enabled

Services (ITES) has helped in improving the picture of our u . S . A . Inside the eyes of the entire globe. Other nations have started thinking about India at par with them on the subject of its provider sectors.

7. **Increase in Exports**- Due to the boom within the provider sectors and the fine of the identical, there has been a excellent growth in the exports of the u. S. A.This in turn is including fast boom and development to the u . S . A. Inside the form of earnings and ranking.
8. **Increase in Number of Working Woman-** Due to the growth inside the service sectors and the employment opportunities inside the equal, it has given sufficient work possibilities to girls too.

COMPONENTS OF SERVICE MARKETING

Your Service and Place

Using your target market is the best way to convey where you are. You must be at the right place at the right time if you want to sell and supply a product or service. Workplaces for lawyers and scientists tend to be located near a courthouse or medical facility. If you're selling a product or service, the appropriate location offers fewer travel time between sales opportunities, as well as the opportunity to be associated with a larger organisation.

The Right People

Having the appropriate employees may make or break a service-based business. A company's success depends on how its employees and managers connect with customers and potential customers. You should create a marketing strategy that promotes your service business personnel, not just your brand. Brand recognition is no longer as important to customers as personal ties with service providers.

Knowledge in Service Marketing

Because of their expertise, service providers are hired. A prominent advertising and marketing tool is information about the company's employees and owners. Consider participating in a discussion on social media, blogs and other marketing tools if you're attending an educational session. Provide information about the education of your services if you are walking a high-end restaurant and offering food and beverage pairings. In this way, serving becomes a joyous experience rather than a chore.

Value over Price

In many cases, the value of a product or service is more important than its price. Consider the cost of the service while developing a marketing strategy for a service-based business. For their customers' benefit, a good services company knows exactly how to fulfil or surpass expectations in terms of price expectations, which they share freely with their customers. Because most customers care about how quickly a service is delivered, advertising and marketing materials should highlight speed over other concerns in order to attract customers.

Relationships in Service

Relationships are the glue that holds people together. Competitive advantage is gained by properly-managed services companies through increasing safety against service problems and opposition, as well as the discovery of new growth opportunities, as a result of relationships. When it comes to client interactions, the supplier organisation must show a high degree of dedication to marketing. The more satisfied your clients are with your service, the less likely they are to remember a rival. Customers are more willing to accept additional revenue opportunities if they feel they are appreciated.

Problem Solving

To be successful, service providers must demonstrate that they can solve their customers' problems rather than providing a one-size-fits-all service. Using this strategy will allow you to rise above the rest of the pack. This includes post-sale customer service, as problems may arise and word-of-mouth classified advertisements still rely on your consumer having an outstanding experience long after the transaction.

Specialization

Customers benefit from more focus since it alleviates stress. Customers want to work with organisations that specialise in a particular service. Specialists are sent to people who are sick and cannot be diagnosed by their primary care physician, reassuring them that their condition may be treated. In order to grow your customer base, you might use specialisation to target a specific problem in your target industry or niche. Specialization gives you more control over your market share since it prevents you from spreading yourself too thinly.

Product

Clients are commonly used as a means of describing a company's products. In order to meet consumer demands, products must be able to bridge the gap between your consultant and the customer. In order to prove that they're listening, service companies create a product message that explains how their customers will benefit. Your services can be used to sell your items; customer service personnel are precise in that they can personalise talks to distinct capacity consumers and actually identify solutions for them.

FACTORS LEAD TO A SERVICE ECONOMY

MEANING OF SERVICE ECONOMY:

As the service sector expands, so does the service zone's duration, which is increasing across the board. Emerging economies are experiencing a surge in service output, which often accounts for at least half of GDP. As a result, the service sector is expanding. The proportion of people employed in agriculture, business, and other sectors will rise in tandem with the development of a national financial system (together with production and mining). In developing countries like India, the provider economic system is typically based on financial, health, and educational services.

FACTORS CONTRIBUTING TO THE GROWTH OF SERVICE SECTOR

1. GOVERNMENT POLICIES:

Rate degree, allocation techniques, and defining technique attributes are all mandated by the government.

The "Privatization" of the government's "rework" groups is another significant measure made by the government.

Transformation of activities like telecommunication and airlines has resulted in a decrease in prices and a more careful approach to market research.

PROS OF PRIVATIZATION:

a. Boost the efficiency

b. Expand in income

New alter will require offerings company to alternate their advertising strategy, operational approaches, and HR guidelines.

2. SOCIAL CHANGES

People are now working in businesses that require them to hire others to fulfil chores once done by a member of their family.

As an illustration, consider child care.

Laundry

Food advising

Increased profits are a combination of living style changes.

Costs are falling for a wide range of high-tech gadgets designed to help people buy for computers.

Cellphones on the go, for example.

3. BUSINESS TRENDS

A large number of professional groups have to comply with the government's demands to lift longstanding restrictions on advertising and promotion.

There has been a wide spread of franchising in a number of service industries.

Independent marketers are licenced to create and advertise a brand-named product in accordance with a set of very specific rules.

4. ADVANCES IN IT:

From the introduction of computers and tele-conversation, the world has changed.

In order to anticipate new trends, segment the market, and find new advertising chances, more influential software allows companies to develop databases that combine information about customers with information about all of their transactions.

Wi-Fi networks and the transfer from cellular phones to laptops and scanners, allowing sales and customer service workers to stay in touch, have been implemented.

5. INTERNATIONALISATION AND GLOBALIZATION:

A strategy for global expansion can be driven by a desire to enter new markets or by a desire to better serve customers who are travelling to other countries in greater numbers.

When companies set up shop in new countries, they frequently choose to work with a small number of global providers rather than a large number of local ones.

The result is an increase in opposition and the transfer of innovation from the United States to the United States of America in every product and procedure.

The growth of this area in India has been influenced by a variety of factors. Affluence is rising, girls' esteem is rising, the IT sector is expanding, markets are developing, health care is becoming more popular, the economic system is being organised, and so on.

MODULE – 2

SERVICE CONSUMER BEHAVIOUR

Consumers want to know about the service's features, advantages, and benefits, as well as how easy it is to use, before making a purchase choice.

People who have a better grasp of consumer behaviour can appreciate the complexity of the decisions that consumers face. In addition, it aids in the identification of our own consumer motivations and decision-making processes, allowing us to make more informed decisions about which goods, services, brands, and establishments to patronise.

Customers, groups, and organisations are all studied in terms of how they buy, use, and discard products and services in order to satisfy their requirements and wants. In this context, it refers to the activities and motivations of consumers in the marketplace.

In order for customers to make a purchasing decision, they first need to identify their needs, obtain relevant information, then weigh their options. Consumer behaviour may be impacted by economic and psychological variables, as well as environmental influences such as social and cultural norms.

When determining what to buy, customers go through a series of steps, including identifying problems, gathering information, weighing options, and finally arriving at a conclusion.

UNDERSTANDING THE CONSUMER DECISION MAKING PROCESS

Because every transaction begins when a consumer realises that they need a product or service, this is the first and most critical step of the buying process.

Customers want to know what their options are throughout this stage of the buying process.

It's at this point in the process when customers are weighing their options and making a decision.

During this stage, the consumer's buying behaviour shifts into action: it's time to buy!

When consumers make a purchase, they assess if they will suggest the product/service/brand to others, if they will purchase it again, and what kind of feedback they will give.

Here are some real-world examples of the many stages in the purchasing decision-making process, along with tips on how your e-commerce brand may get the best outcomes at each level.

1. Need recognition (awareness)

The need recognition stage of the consumer decision making process starts when a consumer realizes a need. Needs come about because of two reasons:

1. Internal stimuli, such as hunger, thirst, illness, exhaustion, melancholy, frustration, etc., are examples of physiological or emotional needs.
2. Extrinsic stimuli, such as a commercial or the fragrance of delectable food.

Most purchases are motivated by physiological or emotional requirements, whether genuine or perceived. This is true even if the primary motivation is vanity or convenience. Social (wanting to look hip and well-dressed) or utilitarian (needing a better computer to accomplish job more successfully) motivations can be behind these stimuli, but they all speak to the same fundamental drivers.

Unless we have food in the house, we will go hungry. Whether it's because we're afraid we'll get cold, or because we're worried we'll be left out of the latest handbag trend, we buy new clothing.

If you're looking for a new camera, an example would be:

What makes someone decide to get a new camera? It's possible that their old camera is broken or they just desire a better one. They may be planning a getaway soon. They might even give the camera to their newlywed sister as a present.

Physiologically, what is the connection between this and a physiological need? Simple. Due to the fact that they can't record their most precious memories otherwise, they feel the need to capture these pleasant times using a camera.

In this circumstance, the internal stimulation is this emotional need. They may not be able to survive without a camera, but they do have a deep emotional need that it addresses.

Do you know what happens once someone points up an issue? They begin to search for a solution right away!" As a result, the following phase in the customer journey is to conduct research.

Secondly, do an investigation (research)

Be present for customers when they start looking for an answer to a problem they've identified! In today's world, where do most people go to find answers? Google!

Researching cameras is an example.

Having realised that a new camera is needed, the customer is now looking for answers. Make sure you're visible to potential customers in this stage.

Consumers may be looking for the following:

- 2020's best cameras
- What's the best camera for the money?

What are the most popular cameras?

How much research a consumer needs to do depends on how familiar he is with the available options, as well as on the complexity of the selections. We may imagine a situation where a person is shopping for a camera as a gift and has no idea what he wants or needs.

He will require more information than someone who already knows exactly what type of camera he wants to buy, but only needs to discover the correct product and the proper manner to buy it..

To a large extent, the amount of time spent looking depends on the specifics of the search.

In other words, how do customers go about finding data? With the use of both internal and external information (their prior understanding of a product or brand) (information about a product or brand from friends or family, reviews, endorsements, press reviews, etc.).

During the stage of need recognition and awareness, the most important thing you can do to optimise your online business is to ensure that you appear in search results and that what the customer sees has an impact.

Efforts to improve the research phase

Make sure your ecommerce shop is optimised to rank for the keywords that are most relevant to your business. Check out our ecommerce SEO guide for more information.

You'll want to make sure your SEO results are optimised to convert once you've learned how to strategize your SEO. During the research stage, you can increase awareness of your business by using user-generated reviews. One of the most efficient methods to accomplish this goal is by this method.

Long-tail keywords are more likely to show up in search results as a result of positive reviews, which can help your store gain visibility. Because they provide a consistent stream of keyword-rich, relevant content, customer reviews boost your website's SEO.

As a result, when someone starts looking for a new camera on their laptop, reviews can help you be there:

3. Taking into account the pros and disadvantages of various options (consideration)

It's time for the customer to analyse their options and see if there are any promising substitutes now that they've done their homework. This is the stage where customers have heard of your brand and have been directed to your website in order to decide whether or not to make a purchase from you.

In order to reduce the risk of making a poor investment, customers base their buying selections on which options are available that best meet their needs.

Two important qualities have an impact on how they are evaluated:

Features, functionality, cost, and ease of use are the four main objectives.

2. Feelings: A brand's reputation (based on previous experience or input from past customers)

Shopping buying a camera can serve as an example of this:

In the consideration stage, your goal is to persuade them that your camera is the best option. You may achieve this by keeping visitors on your site longer and finding strategies to build their trust.

Consumers will initially consider the camera's technical specifications. Are there any features I'm missing? Can you utilise it easily? Do I have enough money to buy it? It's then up to others to decide whether or not it has all the features it should. If so, how difficult was it to learn how to use for others who purchased it? Has anyone had any issues with the product's quality or value for the price

You only get one chance to make a first impression, so seize the moment. Of course, it's critical that your website is informative, your prices are reasonable, and your value is obvious. The word of prior consumers is what sets you distinct if you are identical to a competition in every manner.

deciding on a purchase (conversion)

Now it's time to make some money. Once the customer has made up his or her mind about what or where he or she wants to buy, the sale is complete and the credit card has been pulled out.

Wait, there's more! That's not going to happen. At this point, it's still possible to lose a customer. At this point, the customer's shopping experience is critical, and it must be as simple as feasible.

Example: Choosing a camera over a checkout line

Let's imagine your consumer has reached the checkout step of his transaction and is reconsidering: A different camera could be an option for the recipient. What if the recipient doesn't want this camera because it lacks a feature? To what extent will it be challenging for the recipient to exchange or return the camera if it doesn't satisfy their needs?

This shopper is most likely to abandon his cart and return to the research phase. ' In the end, it's possible he'll find his way back to your site. At this point, your job is to persuade him to make the buy so that you don't lose him for good.

Techniques for increasing conversion rates

Reviews are often included on checkout pages by many businesses. In the right hands, this may be a powerful tool. You must work to earn the customer's confidence, but don't get in the way of the sale.

To display user-generated content during checkout, use site reviews rather than customer images or product reviews, and make sure they aren't clickable. You don't want to be distracted from your goal of creating trust.

After-sale evaluation is the fifth step (re-purchase)

Consumers ponder their most recent purchase at this point in the decision-making process. Consider how they feel about it, whether or not it was a wise buy, and whether or not they will use the brand again in the future or suggest it to family and friends.

Post-purchase strategy is critical in this stage, since it increases the possibility that customers will engage with your business again in the future. Make sure you don't miss out on this highly lucrative opportunity to enhance your eCommerce conversion rate by turning clients into repeat purchasers. Return customers account for around one third of a store's overall revenue on average.

Examples include asking customers for comments and encouraging them to return to the store.

If you've already sold a camera to the consumer, they'll be reviewing their purchase in the example. This is the time when people are most likely to write a review of their trip. This is also the time of year when they are most likely to be receptive to long-term engagement initiatives from your company.

Your goal is to keep consumers coming back and to encourage them to post user generated content (UGC) that will benefit other customers in the future.

Techniques for increasing conversion rates

If you ask for a review, your consumer is much more likely to provide one than if they do it on their own. This is a great way to get valuable feedback from your consumers, as well as useful user-generated content that you can then use to attract new customers in the future.

Consider the fact that your clients have already given you a priceless commodity: their money! It's a good idea to not ask for too much feedback. Encourage customers to submit feedback by making the process as simple as possible for them:

CUSTOMER PURCHASE RISK

It is possible for a consumer to perceive a potential hazard or likelihood of loss when making a transaction. This type of risk To help them decide whether or not to purchase a riskier product, many people talk to relatives and friends or industry professionals before making a purchase.

Risks of financial, physical and performance, time loss, psychological or missed opportunity are among the most frequently discussed in academic literature. At any one time, and for any given item or service, they can occur in various combinations and at various levels.

Perceived risk, according to Arrow (1950), Humphreys and Kenderdine (1979) and Taylor (1975), "represents an uncertain, probabilistic prospective future outlay." Perceived risk can be defined as the uncertainty customers feel before making a purchase of a product or service. In marketing and sales, the word "perceived risk" refers to the customer's impression of the hazards connected with any transaction, particularly those that are expensive, complex, or feature-rich, such as computers and laptops.Perceived risk can be of different types.

Listed below are the various types of Perceived risk.

1. Functional Risk

A functional risk is a risk that affects the product's ability to function. As an example, a person who enjoys baking cakes for his family and friends would wonder, "Will the oven be able to bake many batches of cakes?" Product features, functions, and perceived benefits are all factors that contribute to functional perceived risk, as are worries about the product's quality.

As a result of the product's features, this type of risk can be easily addressed by the parent company. Such perceived risks can be alleviated if proper product information is provided and every customer question is answered.

2. Physical Risk

Physical dangers include concerns regarding the product's safety. When a customer is unsure about the safety of a product or service, he or she may hesitate to make a purchase.

In this case, the parent company may simply relieve the customer's anxieties by providing information about the safety of the product. For instance, the customer's reservations about using the microwave oven would be a simple example of this. Consumers are understandably concerned about the safety of cooking in a microwave after numerous studies have shown that microwave radiation can have a negative impact on health. The manufacturing company can explain how the food is safe when cooked in a certain material in order to put this anxiety to rest.

3. Financial Risk

Return on Investment (ROI) is an indicator of financial perceived risk. Assessing the value of the goods they intend to buy and determining if it outweighs their investment are two examples of Financial perceived risks. Buying something on the spur of the moment can be financially risky for consumers who are concerned about losing money.

A good illustration of this would be a buyer debating if the USD 525 dishwasher he plans to buy is worth the money. The manufacturing firm can also address this type of risk by providing information about the product – such as its life expectancy.

4. Social/psychological Risk

Creating a brand identity and image that customers can identify with is a well-known reality in the business world. In the same way that customers begin to link themselves with a particular brand, so they are reluctant to associate themselves with a newer or lower-cost brand.

Perceived dangers like these fall under the heading of "Social risk." Wearing a particular brand of clothing can lower one's social status, for instance. An further example of a customer's concern about perceived social risk is whether a particular high-priced outfit will be approved by their parents, or even if a particular brand of dinnerware will complement their classy and expensive dining set.

5. Time risk

When acquiring a new product, consumers may be concerned about the amount of time it will take them to use it. The consumer here is concerned about the amount of time and effort the new product will take up.

There are many examples of this, such as when a company replaces its old software with a newer one. The company would have to invest time and effort in training its employees to use the new software if it were to do so. These concerns can be addressed by marketing products as time savers.

Because consumers' purchasing decisions are influenced by their perceptions of danger, companies in a wide range of industries are doing everything they can to alleviate customer anxiety. When it comes to resolving consumer concerns about perceived hazards, some popular solutions include providing warranties and guarantees, providing thorough information about their product, or enlisting the assistance of well-known celebrities.

CUSTOMER EVALUATION

The review of each quality criterion identifies the specific parts of the service delivery process that require improvement. Statistics and graphs are used to evaluate the measurement findings, and correlation analysis is used to discover the relationship between the quality standards.

Customer service evaluations are critical to ensuring that consumers get the information and assistance they need. Customer service evaluation methods are used across a wide range of industries, but contact centres and other firms that place a high value on customer service are the most common. Managers and decision-makers might benefit from a better understanding of the many methods for evaluating customer service.

Every day, customers have to decide what they're going to buy and where they're going to buy it. Businesses must make sure their customers are happy in order to keep them coming back. How do you know when a customer is satisfied? Where do you keep clients in an ever-changing marketplace?

When done correctly, evaluation can aid in issue solving, decision making, and information accumulation. There are many different types of evaluation, but the goal is always the same: to gain a better knowledge of how to enhance health care.

CUSTOMER EXPERIENCE

In general, four main factors influence consumers' experience, involvement, and satisfaction with a product:

Personal: Personal views, attitudes and values have a significant impact on a person's interactions with products and services. Some cultures prevent women from showing particular areas of their bodies as a religious belief, which has a direct impact on their clothing consumption. Language, mythology, conventions, rituals, and laws are further examples of cultural influences. It is common for consumers who believe a product is able to fulfil their own wants to get more invested in it. There are several personal or individual elements that can have a significant impact on a person's life, including gender, age, income, ethnicity, and sexual orientation.

Object: Consumers' experience, involvement, and contentment can be influenced by the amount of information they have about a product, as well as how well they can differentiate its qualities. The more knowledgeable a consumer is about a product, the more likely they are to engage with it. The more information a buyer has about a product, the more essential it becomes to them, especially if some of that information refers to personal qualities.

Situational: Consumers are more likely to use products that can readily fit into and enhance their lifestyles. Smart phones may be used by busy mothers, for example, to keep them organised and productive in a simple manner.

Social: Consumers' purchasing decisions are heavily influenced by social norms, particularly when it comes to the things they select and purchase. Customers' social networks have a significant impact on the products they use, as people prefer to rely on the advice and opinions of their friends and relatives. Opinion leaders and reference groups are two more social forces that might have an impact.

What is the significance of assessing customer service?

Evaluating customer service is important for several reasons, including:

Improving processes

You may improve your procedures by evaluating your customer service. You may be able to make better decisions regarding your rules and processes if you can spot patterns in your customer service. Customers are more likely to be satisfied when businesses follow these trends. It is possible to enhance income, improve brand reputation, and increase client retention through increasing customer satisfaction levels.

Communicating appreciation

You may be able to express your gratitude to your clients by promoting superior customer service. The more delighted your customers are with your company, the more likely they are to spread the word about your products and services to their friends and colleagues. This can help you grow your consumer base and retain good interactions with your present clients.

Tracking business decisions

Even while you make changes to your processes, it's a good idea to keep an eye on customer service. In order to make better selections, you should keep track of your company decisions and how they affect customer service. To improve customer service and meet client needs, you can use this information to make better business decisions.

WAYS TO EVALUATE CUSTOMER SERVICE

1. First call resolution

First call resolution is a metric you can use to measure how frequently your customer service representatives resolve issues within one phone call. If agents resolve problems within a single call, customers may feel more satisfied with customer service. High rates of first call resolution often indicate efficiency and knowledge of your products and services within your customer care team.

2. Customer waiting time

The amount of time a client has to wait on hold before being contacted by a customer service representative is referred to as customer waiting time. Reviewing your average hold time might help you determine how soon your consumer receives information and attention. Your customer service may suffer if clients are on hold for too long. It is possible that the number of customer care agents, volume of calls, and the expertise of your employees can all affect client wait times.

3. Customer greeting

How customer service representatives greet employees is an important aspect to consider when evaluating the quality of your customer service. Successful customer greetings often include clear easily understood tone of voice, an introduction of the speaker and the company and a phrase that makes the customer feel valued and acknowledged. To implement successful customer greetings, consider writing a script or template that your customer service agents can refer to.

4. Problem-solving skills

The ability to quickly solve problems is a trait many customer service professionals may benefit from developing. Be sure to include problem-solving skills in your performance reviews to understand and foster the skills of your employees. It may also be beneficial to provide training and exercises that help your team members prepare to take initiative and resolve issues independently and to the point of customer satisfaction.

5. Product knowledge

Customer service representatives that are well-versed about their products and services are more likely to be successful in their roles. In addition to benefiting the customer, well-trained customer service representatives help their employer by maintaining a high standard of excellence and enhancing the company's reputation. If you want to know how well your employees know about your products and services, you can conduct regular assessments and add occasional training sessions to keep your employees up to date.

6. Customer handover rates

Sometimes, a customer service representative may need to escalate a service call or ticket to another individual or department.

When this happens, it's considered a customer handover. Customer handovers are often necessary and can help to resolve a situation, but too many handovers may make the customer feel impatient or frustrated. To evaluate handover rates, consider implementing a tracking system by requiring team members to document each instance of customer handover.

7. Length of call time

Length of call time is a valuable metric because it can help you understand how quickly your customers receive the information or solutions they need. Consider collecting data about the length of each call and finding the average length for all calls. Typically, shorter call time indicates high-quality customer service. Consider making average call time goals for each month to motivate your employees to complete calls as efficiently as possible.

8. Customer complaints

The amount of customer complaints you receive can be a direct correlation to your customer service. Consider tracking the amount of complaints you receive each day or during calls with your customer service representatives. You can do this using a voice analytics software that can alert you to certain keywords associated with dissatisfied customers. Then, consider finding trends or common sources for complaints to determine how to improve your processes.

9. Abandoned calls

Abandoned calls are calls that customers leave before completion. This could happen because of long waiting times or frustration with automated phone menus. Measuring if and how frequently this occurs can help you determine barriers and challenges your representatives may face and find solutions.

10. Resolved tickets

Your customer service professionals' success can be measured by comparing the number of service tickets to the number of resolved tickets. Compare the number of service tickets received over a period of time with the number of tickets that were resolved to get this information. Viewing the types of tickets that routinely go unanswered can help you identify areas for improvement. Increasing your product and service knowledge may help you resolve more tickets.

11. Success rate of calls

Customer complaints, problems, and inquiries must be resolved in order for a call to be considered successful. You may learn a lot about your customer service by keeping track of how many of your calls are answered. Your product and service knowledge, your ability to communicate with customers, and the effectiveness of your customer care team could all fall under this category. Record the outcomes of your team's calls to get information on this statistic.

12. Tone and language

The tone and language your customer service personnel use with your customers is a critical component of providing good customer service.. You can search for keywords that match the language you want your representatives to use using speech recognition software. Customer service personnel could also benefit from using a script or template to ensure that they are welcoming, appreciated, and valued at all times.

13. Cross-selling opportunities

Cross-selling refers to offering an additional product or service that may meet your customers' needs. Measuring how frequently your representatives use cross-selling techniques could provide insight into how thoroughly they meet customer needs and preferences. To track this information, you may implement a policy that requires employees to record and document instances of cross-selling.

14. Immediate response rate

Immediate response rate refers to the ratio of customers that connect with a representative without waiting versus the amount of customers that wait on hold before speaking with a representative. This information is important to evaluating customer service because it helps you understand how effectively your response team completes their duties. If your ratio indicates high numbers of waiting customers, it may indicate barriers or challenges your representative's face. Understanding the cause of delays can help you eliminate or lower waiting time for your customers.

15. Response to training

Response to training refers to how well representatives and team members apply the lessons learned from training to their daily customer interactions. This is another instance where voice analytic software may be a beneficial tool to scan for keywords and communication techniques included in your organization's training. You may also listen to conversations between newer representatives and customers to evaluate their success applying their training to real-life scenarios.

16. Customer satisfaction

Often, customer happiness is a good measure of how well your customer service is being delivered to your customers. You can find out if your customers are happy by asking them to fill out surveys or by reading online reviews. Customers' satisfaction can be tracked using one of these two approaches. This data can be used to inform policy and practise changes that will better serve your customers.

17. Referrals

Referral rates are how frequently your customers find your products and services thanks to a referral from someone they know. This can give you insight into the overall satisfaction of your customers by providing metrics about their willingness to recommend your offerings. To gather this information, consider including questions about referrals in your customer surveys or market research.

18. Customer retention rate

Customer retention rate refers to how many of your customers repeat purchases of your products and services. Customer retention rate can provide information about customer satisfaction and how well your products, services and team members meet the needs of your customers. To measure customer retention, consider reviewing the number of repeat purchases you receive within a certain amount of time and monitoring these numbers to identify trends.

TIPS FOR EVALUATING CUSTOMER SERVICE

Below are some additional tips to help you evaluate customer service:

Ask for customer feedback

Asking for customer feedback about how you could improve your customer service can provide you with direct insight into your customers' perspectives. To do this, consider including a section of your customer surveys that asks customers how you could improve your products and services. Then, try to take this information into account when strategizing ways to improve your customer service.

Use mystery shoppers

Mystery shoppers are individuals of your organization that enter your stores or establishments to monitor customer and employee interaction. You can use mystery shoppers to gain first-hand observations of your customer service in real-life scenarios. This information can help you identify barriers, challenges and trends within your customer service techniques and help you make improvements where needed.

Review written correspondence

Reviewing the written correspondence between your employees and customers can help you monitor customer service. Consider reviewing emails, instant messages and other forms of written communication to ensure your employees use the language, tone and techniques needed to provide excellent customer service. This can help you identify trends and employees who may need additional guidance and training.

CONSUMER DECISION PROCESS IN SERVICES MARKETING

Knowledge of the Buyer

In buying decisions a lot of times other people also control the decision. In services these roles are played by many persons. In purchase of any service six different roles are played. They are;

- **Initiator**: The person who has a specific need and proposes to buy a service
- **Influencer:** The person or group of persons whom the decision maker refers to or who advice the decision maker
- **Gate Keeper**: The person or organization or promotional material, which act as filter on the range of services which enter the decision choice
- **Decider** : The person who makes the buying decision
- **Buyer** : The person makes the actual purchaser
- **User** : The actual user.

CONSUMER DECISION MAKING PROCESS IN SERVICES MARKETING

The moment of truth for a marketer comes when a customer decides whether or not to purchase or reject a product or service. It's a good sign if the marketing approach was well-thought out and on target, or a bad sign if it wasn't. Because of this, marketers are very interested in the process by which a customer chooses an option from among a variety on offer. There is also the option of not making a purchase at all.

An easy-to-understand model for consumer decision-making connects together psychological, social, and cultural themes. Input variables, process variables, and output variables make up the three categories of variables in the decision model.

Input Variables: Input variables are those variables which affect the decision making process and include commercial marketing efforts as well as non-commercial influences from the consumer's socio-cultural environment.

Decision Variables: The decision process variables are influenced by consumer's own psychological fields, which affect their recognition of a need, their pre-purchase search for information and their evaluation of alternatives.

Output Variables: The output phase of the model includes the actual purchase (either trial or repeat purchase) and post purchase evaluation. Both pre-purchase and post-purchase evaluation feed back in the form of experience into the consumer's psychological field and serves to influence future decision processing. (On a holiday a customer may change hotels in between his stay).

FACTORS INFLUENCING THE CONSUMER BUYING BEHAVIOR ARE

- **Situational Factors:** Time, Store's atmosphere, Marketing Stimuli (the occasion)
- **Personal Factors:** Personality, life style, other demographic factors like age, gender, occupation etc.
- **Social Factors: Culture, reference group, family.**
- **Psychological Factors**: Perception, attitude, motivation.

CONSUMER EXPECTATION

Consumer expectations are based on the economic outlook of families. People are more likely to take out loans and purchase things if they believe the economy will improve.

When a consumer uses a product or service, what they expect to happen is what they call customer expectations.

Consumers research and interpret the product's features, which affects their perception of the product's quality. Expectations from customers may include their intended outcomes from using a product. It's possible that a product they wish to like and like the brand has high expectations because of this.

Why are customer expectations important?

Customer expectations are important because they can:

- **Affect your brand reputation**: Customers who perceive your products or services as high performing may also have positive thoughts about your professional brand altogether.
- **Increase brand loyalty:** Exceeding your customers' expectations can inspire them to make future purchases from your brand.
- **Influence product sales**: Customers who have high expectations about your products or services may choose to shop with your brand, helping you increase profits and meet sales goals.
- **Stand out against competitors**: With satisfaction and loyalty to your brand, customers may recommend your products or services to other customers, which allow you to stand out against competitors.

How do customers form their expectations?

Customers form their expectations in the following ways:

Experience

A customer's expectations are shaped by their prior use of similar products or services like yours. Clients may have high expectations for the quality of your leather furniture if they purchased leather furniture in the past and consider it a wise investment.

Knowledge

As a result, customers may be able to forecast the product or service's quality based on their prior knowledge. For example, an esthetician would consider purchasing a well-known beauty brand's skincare product. To ensure that a product works as advertised, estheticians advise their clients to check over the ingredients list before purchasing to ensure that the product is safe and effective for their skin type.

Interactions with the organization

Product expectations are based on the brand's interactions with its customers. People expect more from brands that they've previously had favourable experiences with. As an example, a chicken sandwich from a fast-food business is being advertised. The consumer is confident that they will appreciate the chicken sandwich because they have had a positive encounter at the restaurant.

External communication

Customers may form their expectations about products or services from the following types of external communication:

Blog posts: To help customers decide whether or not to purchase a product, they may read blog entries that detail the product and what they may expect from using it. It's common for people to see a blog post about the benefits of sugar waxing and how it's most successful at hair removal, which raises their expectations of how sugar waxing will assist them.

Online customer reviews: In order to make a purchasing decision, shoppers can look at other people's reviews of the products in question. If a product has a lot of positive evaluations from other customers, it may be perceived as high-quality by potential consumers.

Social media commentary: Customers' perceptions of a product's quality can be influenced by its popularity on social media. Prospective buyers may have high expectations for a new mobile app if a large number of people on social media are enthusiastic about it.

Celebrity endorsements: In order to get their admirers to buy a product or service, celebrities leverage their celebrity status and likeness. Customers may have high expectations for a perfume's scent, for example, if a well-known pop celebrity has declared it to be their favourite.

SERVICE SATISFACTION

The word "customer satisfaction" refers to the degree to which customers are pleased with a company's goods, services, and other offerings. Information from surveys and ratings can assist a company decide how to improve or alter its products and services.

Getting what you sought or desired or paying off a debt gives you a sense of fulfilment. When you have a decent job and a happy marriage, you feel satisfied. One way to feel satisfied is to pay off all of your credit card debt.

Customer satisfaction relates to how successfully you, as a product or service provider, meet your consumers' requirements and expectations. This applies to both pre- and post-sale interactions, as well as during the sale. ... "An indicator of how satisfied customers are with a company's service."

WHY IS CUSTOMER SATISFACTION IMPORTANT?

High levels of customer satisfaction and loyalty go hand in hand. Retaining existing customers is critical to a company's capacity to remain viable in the long term. However, metrics such as sales and shares can disclose crucial information about how a firm is now functioning, but customer satisfaction levels are a better predictor of future performance.

1. CSAT identifies your unsatisfied customers

As a business owner, it is imperative that you identify and deal with consumers that are unsatisfied. The longevity of a business might be jeopardised by negative customer reviews or word-of-mouth cautions to friends and family based on bad experiences. Customers will know that you value their opinions if you regularly conduct surveys and respond to any negative comments with solutions and improvements. The more you show your dissatisfied consumers how much you care about them, the more likely they are to come back.

2. CSAT identifies your happy customer

In order to expand your company, you must place a high value on ensuring that your clients are happy. Customers' satisfaction levels must be assessed and analysed in order to establish whether or not they are content. It's crucial to have happy consumers since they'll stick around and spread the word about your business. If you want to encourage these customers to bring in additional recommendations and advertise on your behalf, you may set up customer advocacy programmes for them.

3. CSAT forecasts help you prioritize.

In order to prioritise your efforts, you can use customer metrics. Client satisfaction data enables your teams to identify the areas in which they need to focus their efforts in order to improve the health of your customer base. Making your customers happy is a joint effort by your customer success teams, sales representatives, production workers, and marketing professionals all across the world.

4. CSAT powers internal processes

Customer satisfaction data reveals who is using your product or service and how satisfied they are with it. Using these metrics appropriately can be extremely beneficial. You may fine-tune your marketing strategies, sales tactics, and other internal processes by getting a better understanding of your consumer base and how satisfied they are with your product.

5. CSAT attracts new leads

Positive feedback from existing customers is a powerful tool for attracting new ones. An rise in favourable evaluations is a direct result of an increase in consumer satisfaction. Many more potential clients will find your business through word-of-mouth recommendations than through any other type of marketing strategy.

6. CSAT sells.

Customers' contentment is a selling element for sales teams. When pitching to new customers, highlighting high customer satisfaction rates is a powerful tool. It's also possible to learn from satisfied customers what aspects of your service or product are unique benefits over your competition.

7. CSAT guides product updates

In the long run, a product's negative reviews can be a good thing. Customers who aren't satisfied with a product or service can open the door to fixing a problem that could affect many others in the future when they express their dissatisfaction. Even more so in the case of firms that frequently upgrades their software and need to repair faults as soon as possible.

SERVICE QUALITY

For every consumer that visits a restaurant or shop, they have an idealised vision of the service they anticipate to receive. How well a service meets consumer expectations is measured by service quality. High-quality service is defined as a company's ability to meet or exceed customer expectations. Fast food restaurants typically serve food within five minutes after ordering, so let's assume that you're going out for dinner. It is only when you have your drink and a table that your order is called! You'd probably classify this as excellent customer service. Customers look at five factors when evaluating the quality of a service. Let's take a closer look at their dimensions.

DIMENSIONS OF SERVICE QUALITY

The Five Dimensions of Service Quality Measured by the SERVQUAL Instrument

The SERVQUAL Instrument measures the five dimensions of Service Quality. These five dimensions are: tangibility, reliability, responsiveness, assurance and empathy.

1. Tangibility

Customers evaluate the quality of a service by comparing the tangible aspects of the service to those of the competition. a company's external image, including its physical assets, staff, and marketing materials, is an important consideration. Survey respondents were asked about FFR's physical layout and amenities, which they provided in their answers on the survey's questionnaire.

2. Reliability

Being able to reliably and accurately deliver on a service's claim is an important quality to have. Delivering on the company's commitments, such as delivery, service provision, problem resolution and price, is what it means to be reliable. If you can't maintain your promises to customers, they won't trust you. Be mindful of what your customers anticipate from your company. Companies who fail to offer the basic service that customers expect to receive fail their customers directly.

3. Responsiveness

You must be ready and able to assist consumers in a timely manner. This aspect focuses on how quickly and attentively a company responds to the needs and concerns of its customers. Customers' perceptions of responsiveness are shaped by the length of time it takes to receive assistance, have their inquiries answered, or have issues addressed. It also encompasses a sense of adaptability and the ability to tailor the service to meet the needs of the customer.

4. Assurance

Confidence and trust are instilled by this. The ability of a company and its personnel to foster a sense of trust and confidence among its employees is what is meant by the term "assurance." Those services that the consumers regard as requiring a high rise and/or that they are unsure of how to evaluate are likely to be of particular importance in this dimension. The individual who connects the customer to the organisation, such as the marketing department, may embody trust and confidence. As a result, staff are aware of the need of building customer trust and confidence in order to achieve a competitive edge and maintain client loyalty.

5. Empathy

It refers to the company's commitment to providing personalised service to its clients. To demonstrate to the consumer that the business is doing its best to meet his demands, certain countries require that each customer receive individualised attention from a representative. Client trust and confidence are increased by empathising with them, and this also helps to build long-term customer loyalty. Consumers' expectations are rising all the time in today's competitive environment, and businesses must do everything in their power to match those expectations. Otherwise, those customers who don't feel valued will go elsewhere.

CUSTOMER HAS NEEDS AND EXPECTATIONS

In order to suit their individual demands, customers purchase goods and services. Many people's needs are firmly ingrained in their subconscious thoughts, and they may have long-term implications and identify issues that affect their lives. When a person has a desire, they are more likely to act on it. Purchasing a product or service is frequently considered as the greatest way to address a specific need. Furthermore, consumers may then evaluate what they received against what they expected, especially if it was more expensive than an alternative option or required more time, money, or effort.

Expectations from customers include a range of service standards that fall somewhere between the ideal and the idealised levels.

Desired and Adequate Service Levels

Desired service refers to the type of service clients expect to obtain. Ideally, it is a blend of what customers believe can and should be supplied in the context of their individual demands. But most people recognise that organisations can't always provide the quality of service they expect; this is described as the minimum amount of service customers may accept without becoming disappointed. Is this expectation based on variables such as the degree of service that can be expected from other providers, as well as the current situation? To some extent, customers' high hopes and low service expectations can be traced back to the provider's verbal and nonverbal promises as well as to the customer's previous experiences.

Predicted Service Level

"Adequate service" is defined in terms of the degree of service customers expect to receive, known as anticipated service. This means that if good service is projected, the adequate level will be higher. Customers' expectations of service may be influenced by the unique circumstances in which they are given.

Zone of Tolerance

Because of the intrinsic nature of services, it can be difficult to provide consistent service from one day to the next, even by the same service person inside the same firm. The "zone of tolerance" refers to the range of acceptable variance for a given consumer base. Customers will be frustrated and dissatisfied if a performance falls below the acceptable service level, however exceeding the required service level would both please and surprise them. To put it another way, you can think of the zone of tolerance as the range of service within which clients aren't particularly concerned about service quality. Positive or negative reactions will occur when service falls outside the acceptable range. Depending on factors including competition, pricing, and the relevance of specific service features, a customer's tolerance level might rise or fall. While appropriate service levels can rise or fall depending on the circumstances, desired service levels rise relatively slowly over time as customers build up a wealth of knowledge and experience.

It is known that expectations are not stable in the sense that they may change over time due to changes in aspiration levels or need at a particular moment in time. Customers' expectations about what constitutes good service vary from one business to another. Expectations are not determined by individuals themselves but also by reference groups, external situations, norms, values, time and service provider. Generally speaking, expectations can be formulated in terms of "what should be done" and in terms of what should be done" Expectations change over time influenced by both supplier-controlled factors such as advertising, pricing, new technologies and service innovation as well as social trends advocacy by consumer organization and increased access to information through the media and the internet.

"Our study demonstrates that customer service expectations exist at two separate levels; a desirable level and an adequate level," state Berry and Parasuraman (1991). The customer's expectations are reflected in the service level. Essentially, it's a combination of what the buyer likes. Part of the reason for this is due to the customer's expectations for the level of service they expect to receive. Zone of tolerance refers to the gap between the targeted service level and the level of adequate service that customers are ready to accept.

MODULE – 3

MANAGING SERVICE ENCOUNTERS

Because service encounters can have a significant impact on consumer satisfaction, they play a major role in the marketing of services (Solomon et al., 1985). Clients' satisfaction is impacted by these factors in addition to service distinction and quality control

In a service encounter, a person (such as a vendor, office clerk, or travel agent) offers another person with a service or good (such as a product, an appointment, or plane tickets).

As any interaction between the consumer and the service provider that is directly related to the supply of the core service, we define a service encounter.

TYPES OF SERVICE ENCOUNTERS

Customers have service encounters whenever they interact with a service provider. Remote encounters, phone encounters, and face-to-face interactions are all sorts of service encounters. A consumer may meet any or all three of these sorts of service interactions when working with a service provider.

The term "Remote Encounter" refers to an encounter that takes place but does not include any direct human contact. Automated dial-in ordering, for example, when a consumer interacts with a bank through an ATM or a mail-order service. The firm's billing bills and other sorts of information are also sent to customers by mail, resulting in remote meetings. Even though there is no direct human interaction in these remote meetings, each represents an opportunity for a company to reaffirm or establish client perceptions. Technical processes and systems, as well as concrete evidence of the service, become the major criteria for determining quality when dealing with a company over the phone. The development of Internet-based apps has made it possible to use technology to deliver services. Internet services include retail purchases, airline ticketing, repair and maintenance issues, and package and shipment tracking. Service interactions of any kind, whether in person or over the phone, are remote encounters.

A phone encounter is a sort of interaction between a consumer and a company that is most common in many organisations. Customers, inquiries, and orders are all handled by phone in almost any company, regardless of whether it is a manufacturer or a service provider. Because of the increased potential for interaction unpredictability, evaluating the quality of phone conversations is different from evaluating the quality of remote conversations. Quality is judged by the tone of voice, employee competence, and efficiency in handling client issues in these contacts.

Encounters face-to-face Lastly, a Face-to-Face Encounter occurs when an employee and a consumer come into direct physical touch. Customers and hotel staff, including receptionists, bellboys, food and beverage servers, and others, interact face-to-face in a hotel. The most difficult part of addressing challenges of face-to-face service equality is figuring out what they are and why they exist. Nonverbal signals such as employee attire and other symbols of service (equipment, instructional pamphlets, physical surroundings) are equally essential as verbal cues in determining quality. During face-to-face contacts, the customer's personal behaviour is a significant factor in establishing exceptional service for herself. Face-to-face meetings are common at Disney theme parks, where customers and ticket-takers, maintenance workers, actors in Disney character costumes, ride attendants, food and beverage waiters, and others come into contact with each other. Customers and IBM salespeople, delivery employees, maintenance representatives, and professional consultants all interact with one other in a business-to-business scenario.

SERVICE FAILURE

In the simplest terms, a service failure occurs when a customer's expectations are not met by the service provided. In most cases, customers expect to be rewarded for their inconvenience in the form of refunds, credits, discounts, or apologies if a service fails to meet their expectations.

It's possible for even the best service firms to experience failures, which may be due to the service not being available at the specified time, it being delivered late or slowly (some times too fast?), the outcome may be inaccurate or badly executed, or the staff may be unpleasant or uncaring. Negative experiences are caused by all of these service failures. They can cause customers to leave, spread the word about their bad experiences, or even file a complaint in the consumer courts if left unaddressed. Customer happiness, loyalty, and bottom-line performance all improve when concerns are resolved effectively, according to research. In the long run, customers who encounter service failures but are happy by the company's attempts at recovery are more likely to stick around.

SERVICE RECOVERY

In theory, clients who are less than completely content with their initial experience are more likely to be satisfied and return than those who have a positive encounter with the company from the get-go. Hotel guests who come and discover that there are no rooms available are an example of this. The front desk agent promptly upgrades this guest to a better room at the same price as a means of recouping their losses. Because of this recompense, the customer is incredibly delighted with this experience, is even more impressed with the hotel than he was before, and swears to remain loyal to the hotel in the future.." This is a logical, but not very rational, conclusion: corporations should intend to disappoint their customers in order to recover and acquire even more devotion from them. Known as the Service Recovery Paradox, this is an interesting concept. The recovery conundrum is more complicated than it first appears. ' When it comes to service, reliability is the most crucial part of quality, and it would be a waste of money to encourage service failure. According to a study, customers are more likely to return to a store if they have had a positive experience in the past. Negative experiences with a firm will have a negative impact on the company's general reputation as well as repurchase inclinations. Negative perceptions can be erased by an exceptional rehabilitation attempt.

A customer's unfavourable service experience can be remedied by contacting them and resolving the issue. Birchbox's Service Recovery Program is an excellent example of service recovery. Customer service representatives at Birchbox have the authority to follow up with clients who had a bad experience with their service. A poor experience can be transformed into an enjoyable one, resulting in client loyalty.

The recovery paradox has been disproved by a recent study. Customers who had experienced a service failure were consistently less satisfied than those who had not, regardless of the extent of the recovery effort. The scale of the service failure in this investigation, a three-hour flight delay, suggests that there is no recovery paradox. There may be no way to recover from this type of failure. If the recovery paradox does exist, "doing it right the first time" is the safest and most effective way to proceed. Every attempt should be taken to recover as quickly as possible in the event of a failure. It may be feasible to witness the recovery paradox in circumstances when the failure can be totally overcome, or where the recovery effort is clearly superior.

HOW CUSTOMERS RESPOND TO SERVICE FAILURE

When customers take action as a result of a service breakdown, there are numerous options available. On-the-spot complaints allow service providers to respond swiftly to unsatisfied customers and prevent unnecessary downtime. For a business, this is the best-case scenario, because it gives them a second chance at their consumer, a chance to keep them as a customer in the future, and the chance to avoid any bad press.

Some customers opt not to openly complain to the supplier, but rather spread poor word of mouth about the company to friends, relatives, and coworkers. As a result, this poor word of mouth can be exceedingly damaging, as it can reinforce the customer's negativism and propagate that negative opinion to others. In addition, the company has no prospect of recovery unless the bad word of mouth is backed by a complaint to the company directly.

When anything goes wrong, customers have a choice of options for how they want to react. Following a failure, it is expected that the consumer will be dissatisfied at some level. A wide range of unpleasant emotions, including anger, disappointment, self-pity, and anxiety, have been linked to service failure. Even if clients remain silent about their displeasure, they will eventually make a decision about whether or not they will stay with the current service or go with a different one.

Service Recovery Strategy

It's called service failure when a business fails to live up to the expectations it sets with customers by not delivering on its commitments. The consequences of a service outage can be even more severe than they were before. In order to keep customers, maintaining them is a major issue, yet service failure functions as a major roadblock. If a company fails to deliver on its promises, the client is entitled to what they were promised.

The client expects customised service.

The customer is looking for a good apologies.

It's important that customers be not made to feel as if they're to blame for the issue. Despite the fact that they are often to blame for a nuisance,

This time around, there are five phases involved in dealing with a service outage. They're listed here.

Apologies and acknowledgement of the fact that this happened.

Listening to what the customers have to say and responding accordingly.

A sensible explanation is better than defending the firm.
Offer a few additional advantages.

Make sure there are no faults this time around so that he may simply forget about the service failure and remain loyal to your company.

In the event of a service recovery, a client is entitled to three shorts of fairness. The details are provided in the paragraphs that follow.

When a service fails, the corporation has a responsibility to acknowledge the client and make things right. Customer dissatisfaction is possible, but the tone and words chosen by the addresser should still be fair and kind.

Reliability of procedures, i.e. being able to gather detailed information about the frequency of service failures or receiving compensation.

The steps required in the process should be as straightforward as possible. If a company's service fails and its procedures become too complicated, it could cause a catastrophe for its customers.

Outcome equity: the company should compensate, arrange for an other form of transportation, or comply with the customer's condition now that they have realised there is a service failure. The customer's needs and the company's policy should be taken into account while determining the final outcome.

PROCESS OF SERVICE RECOVERY

1. Apologize. Apologizing does not suggest that you are blaming yourself; rather, it means that you are accepting that the other person is not satisfied with your performance.

Identify the Issue. You must first refrain from taking conclusions and suspend your judgement.

Second, pay attention. Make sure you're on the same page as your consumer by verifying that you comprehend what they are saying. Finally, inquire about the information you need.

Find out what happened. In this case, it's not necessary for your consumer to know this information. Customers may interpret the explanation as blaming the company. A person's credibility is harmed when they assign blame. In order to prevent it from happening again, it is necessary to identify the 'source' of the problem. What if there's a problem with the way things are being done? Is it something to do with the way things are being done?

Provide a few options. There is always the option of doing nothing. Your customer and you can come up with any other solutions. If it's suitable, brainstorm with your consumer to find a solution. Ultimately, you want to provide customers with a variety of options and empower them to make their own decisions. As long as your customer is aware of the additional fees involved, don't be hesitant to present them as an option.

Implementation of the Solution is the fifth step. Do all in your power to make sure that the customer's solution is implemented in a timely manner.

Thank Them. Customers don't want to be praised for their complaints, therefore don't do it! There's so much potential in this. As a matter of fact, thank you for bringing this to our attention.

"I appreciate your candour," for example.

"Thank you for your ongoing support and confidence."

Thank you for giving us a chance to put things right. "

Check back in. Check in with your customer at the end of the day, if at all possible. Isn't this a great way to show that you're invested in the situation?

CUSTOMER RETENTION

Customer retention refers to a company's ability to keep customers loyal and keep them from switching to a rival company. It tells you if your product and service meet the needs of your current clients. In contrast to customer acquisition or lead creation, customer retention is a distinct process.

Retaining consumers raises the lifetime value of your customers and enhances your revenue. It's also a great way to create strong consumer ties. You're more than just a website or a storefront. They put their trust in you because you provide them with something of worth in return.

In marketing, customer retention is the process of re-engaging customers who have already purchased from you. Because you've already converted the consumer at least once, this isn't customer acquisition or lead creation.

The greatest customer retention strategies allow you to build long-term relationships with your customers, resulting in brand loyalty. They could even become brand advocates if they spread the word throughout their own circles of influence.

BENEFITS OF CUSTOMER RETENTION

1. Retention is Cheaper than Acquisition

But even while "it costs five times as much to gain a new customer" may not be correct in every circumstance, it is still true that keeping a customer costs less than acquiring a new one.

The economics favour data retention as the more economically viable priority even if you still require data, as there has been lots of research into data collection vs. retention.

2. Loyal Customers are More Profitable

Loyalty is not only more cost-effective, but it also provides superior returns. Consumers who are actively involved in a brand's marketing are five times more likely to make repeat purchases, buy 90 percent more frequently, and spend 60 percent more each transaction. They're generating 23% more income and profit than the average consumer on average.

While it is more profitable to have repeat consumers, don't take that for granted. Consider raising pricing if you think they'll remain around for a long period of time, but don't go overboard. A company's long-term financial success is more important than its short-term financial success.

Think about the other side of the coin: "Actively disengaged" clients can cost a business up to 13 percent of its income.

3. Your Brand Will Stand Out from the Crowd

Consider how many brands you interact with that seem to respect your patronage when you put on your consumer hat.

Only a few examples come to mind.

Retention-focused brands stand out from the rest of the pack because most brands are focused on acquiring new customers.

Most people only interact with a small percentage of the 10,000 marketing messages they see every single week. The people that keep their attention are those with whom they have some sort of emotional connection.

The top brands don't have a unique selling offer; they have a distinctive strategy for retaining customers.

4. You'll Earn More Word of Mouth Referrals

New clients will come from repeat customers. When it comes to making purchases, consumers are more likely to trust recommendations from their friends and family than anything else. 90 percent of millennials will spread the word about a brand's adventures through social media.

5. ENGAGED CUSTOMERS PROVIDE MORE FEEDBACK

A company's ability to adapt and grow depends on its employees' ability to provide feedback.

It's common for customers to give brands a chance when they leave comments. They're advising you how to keep earning their trust. People who have complained and had their issue resolved are 84% less inclined to cut back on spending. Please contact us if you need assistance in dealing with customers who post negative reviews. This information is worth your time.

6. Customers Will Explore Your Brand

What an elegant way to explain that you'll be able to sell them more products! Customers are six times more likely to say they'd try a new product or service from a brand if it's already established itself with an existing product or service.

These people can help with #5 above as beta testers, which is an important factor in product development as well as being helpful for sales.

7. Loyal Customers are more forgiving

More than $1.6 trillion is wasted each year due to customers leaving after a bad experience, according to an Accenture report. In fact, it has been ranked as the most common reason people provide for abandoning a brand. But devoted clients will tolerate some transgressions if they don't happen too often.

8. Customers Will Welcome you're Marketing

No one enjoys being targeted by commercials. With the exception of devoted clients! In fact, they are four times more likely to indicate that they "appreciate when this brand reaches out to me" and seven times more probable that they "always respond to this company's promotional offers."

9. Loyal customers yield higher profits

Customers that remain loyal to a company's brand are more valuable to that company's bottom line. These clients buy more frequently and spend a lot of money every time they do business with them. Even if a brand raises its prices, loyal customers are less likely to switch brands. However, companies must exercise caution while raising their pricing because the end goal is not just today's revenue but revenue over the long term as well.

10. Better communication with customers

Businesses can use customer retention to build a strong relationship with their customers. Customers that have a long-term relationship with a business are more likely to provide helpful feedback. They help businesses understand what customers want and expect from them so that they can create effective policies.

MODULE – 4

SERVICES MARKETS SEGMENTATION

Segmentation is the process of splitting a market into distinct client groups. The next step is to determine which possible consumer categories the organisation will focus on when it comes to target marketing. It comes before targeting and aids a business in being more choosy about the people to whom it markets its goods. For a firm to be successful, both marketing segmentation and targeted marketing are essential. It's common practise in today's marketing to use STP (Segmentation, Targeting, and Positioning). For creating marketing communications plans, the STP model is effective in that it helps marketers to define strategies, then create relevant messages to communicate with diverse audiences.

Market segmentation is the practise of collecting clients with similar needs, wants, preferences, or purchasing habits.. In order to target a certain market segment, a company must first assess the market's attractiveness. In other words, segmentation is a study of customers, while targeting is a decision regarding which customers to service. Effective market positioning necessitates the creation or adaptation of a service mix that is tailored to the customer's perception of the service's competitive position.

The segmentation process, shown in the following figure is concerned to divide a heterogeneous follows four broad steps:

Once the market segment has been selected, the process of target marketing involves developing a positioning for the target segments selected and then developing a marketing mix for each target market.

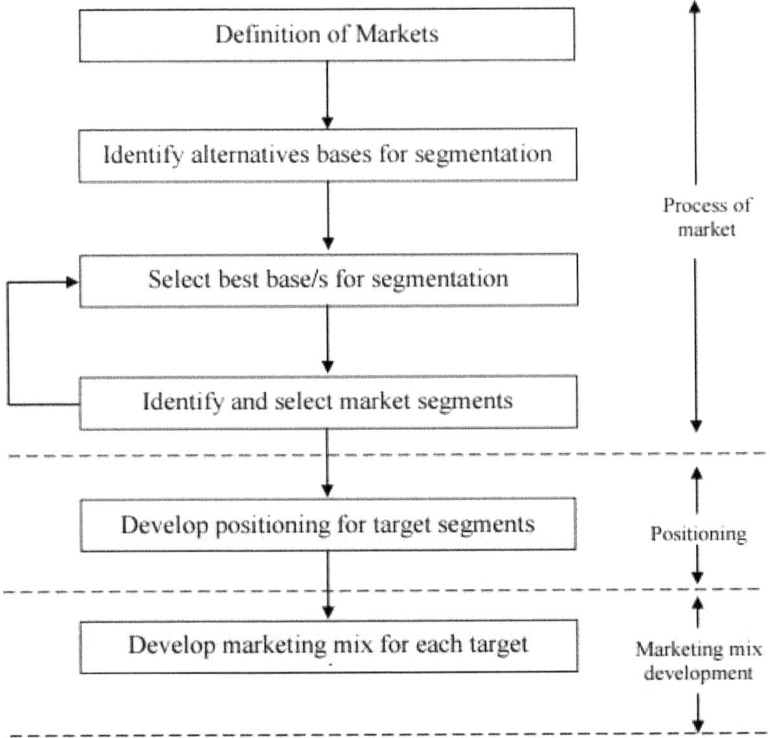

Fig. 5.1 Services market segmentation

Definition of Relevant Market

Definition of the target client group is an important part of marketing a company's products and services. Customers of a certain supermarket in a particular region can be considered a broad group, but they can also be broken down into more specialised subgroups.

Segmenting the market effectively entails catering to the demands of both current and potential customers. This necessitates an in-depth knowledge of client attitudes, preferences, and desired outcomes. The initial stage in the segmentation process is to define the target market and its needs.

Bases of Segmentations

Market segments are formed by grouping customers who share common characteristics that are in some way meaningful to the design, delivery, promotion, or pricing of the service.

Demographics and socio-economic segmentation

Demographic segmentation encompasses a variety of elements, such as gender, age, family size, and other demographic characteristics.. Socioeconomic characteristics, including income education, social class, and ethnic origins, can also be taken into account. Many retail establishments cater to a variety of demographics.

Psychographic segmentation

This type of segmentation is difficult to quantify because it is based on people's habits and lifestyles.

Geographic segmentation

Geographic segmentation divides customers according to where they live or work and correlates this with other variables.

A geographic analysis is a relatively simple means of segmenting a market, it is frequently one of the first segmentation variables to be considered by a service firm Geographic segmentation dimensions are typically grouped into market scope factor and geographic market measures.

1. Market scope factors include a consideration of where the markets to be served are located: this maybe local, national, regional or global.

2. Geographic market measures include examination of population density, climate-related factors, and standardized market areas. Geographic measures are especially important in the selection of specialized mass communications media.

Benefit segmentation

The segmentation variables listed above focus on the personal attributes of the customer. Segmentation can also be carried out on the basis of the customer"s response.

Usage segmentation

The nature and scope of usage patterns are the primary considerations in usage segmentation. Customers are often categorised into heavy, medium, or occasional users of the service being considered.

Promotional response segmentation

Segmenting based on client response to a particular promotional tactic is known as promotional response segmentation. It's possible that this includes a response to marketing efforts such as advertisements, sales promotions, in-store displays, and exhibitions.

Segmentation by service

One area that has received less study is how customers react to different service offerings.

A service-based market segmentation strategy must consider the following concerns, among others:

Is it possible to identify groups of clients with comparable service needs?

Is it possible for us to offer a unique product or service?

Has the same service standard been applied to every product we have to offer?

Examples of the most common types of segmentation employed by service providers may be found in the examples above. However, they are by no means comprehensive. It is expected that the segmentation procedure will lead to one of the following decisions:

It is possible that the service company has decided to focus on a specific market sector.

There may be multiple categories that the service company wants to target, therefore it will create separate marketing mix plans for each one.

The service may be offered to the whole public if management decides not to segment the market. If the market is really tiny and a single chunk would not be viable, this may be the best option. Alternatively, the service provider may have a monopoly on the market, making it impossible to raise volume or profit by focusing on a few niches.

You can discover there is no market fit for your service offering after conducting a thorough market analysis.

The importance of market segmentation in the service sector is becoming more widely accepted.

IMPORTANCE OF SEGMENTATION OF SERVICES

According to previous statements, segmentation is the foundation of good marketing strategies. Market segmentation can also be used to make decisions about the intensity of marketing in specific segments.

Businesses and customers alike can benefit from a segment-based marketing strategy.

1) Focus of the Company – Using this strategy, a company may better target specific market segments. The more focused a marketer is, the more successful he will be. Several automakers have turned their attention to the subcompact car market. Only a corporation that wants to improve its bottom line is making this kind of shift. As a result, businesses construct their plans around a new market segment that has the potential to boost their bottom line.

2) Increase in competitiveness – Marketers' ability to compete in a certain market segment will rise in direct proportion to their increased concentration on that market. A company's competitiveness is enhanced by segmentation. For example, if your target demographic is children and teenagers, your brand's recognition and equity will be high among them. Your share of the market may rise, while the likelihood of a new competitor coming may fall. Customers will be more loyal to the brand as a result. A company's overall competitiveness is also enhanced by market segmentation.

3) Market expansion- It is immediately feasible to expand in segmentation. After a certain territory is served, you can quickly expand to a neighbouring one, if your market strategy is focused on geography. Reebok's expansion into fitness clothing and accessories is an example of a company's ability to target clients based on demographics (Ex – Reebok targets fitness aficionados). Segmentation is critical to growth.

4) Customer retention – It is possible to encourage client retention throughout the course of a customer's lifetime by segmenting your marketing efforts. The Hospitality industry includes everything from hotels to airlines to hospitals, to name just a few examples. In India, the growing industry of hospitality services offers customers a wide range of options, ranging from a small local Dhaba to a five-star luxury hotel, depending on their specific needs.

5) Have better communication – STP is a critical component of the marketing mix's Promotion or communication component. A company's messaging must be precise in order to reach its intended audience. Thus, if you want to target a specific group of people, you need to segment your market. It is impossible to communicate effectively if you do not understand your intended audience. Imagine if you had to explain politics to someone who was on the other side of a curtain. You'd go on and on about political parties, states, countries, and so forth. A 5-year-old child appears over the curtain as soon as you remove the curtain. Is there any use in discussing politics with him? This demonstrates the need for separation in communication. You can't craft a message for your target audience if you don't understand their demographics, psychology, or where they come from.

6) Increases profitability – Increased competition, remember, brand equity, customer retention, and communications can be achieved by segmentation. As a result, if so many aspects of your business are affected, then the profitability of the company is also affected. In the showrooms of Nike, Gucci, or BMW, we never see anyone haggling. Segmentation is one of the brand's main selling points. They're actually aiming for people who don't need to bargain or negotiate. As a result, they enjoy significant levels of profitability.

TARGETING OF SERVICES

When a corporation has a specific group of clients in mind for whom it intends to promote its goods and services, it is said to have a target market. Prior to creating a marketing strategy, the marketer must first determine their target audience. By geography, purchasing power, and psychographics, a target market can be distinguished from the general market.

Once the segments have been evaluated the market to be targeted can be selected on the basis of:

Undifferentiated marketing: Instead of focusing on a specific subset of the target market, an undifferentiated marketing plan targets the entire market. To reach as many people as possible in the target market, this strategy relies on a single marketing mix, consisting of a single product, a single price, a single location, and a single kind of promotion. In their book, "Marketing," William M. Pride and O. Sugar and salt, according to C. Ferrell, are good examples of commodities that could benefit from an undifferentiated marketing strategy because so many people on the market have the same demand for them.

Differentiated marketing: This is a personalised approach that caters to the needs of each individual customer. With a targeted marketing strategy, you can target certain market segments with targeted marketing mixes. For each segment, the mix contains a product that is priced, positioned, and promoted in a way that is tailored to their needs. Segmenting customers by gender is a common practise for companies that provide vitamins. It might make a multivitamin for ladies and a multivitamin for males separately. Segmenting the gender groupings by life stage and designing distinct marketing mixes for each one could help further differentiate. Markets with clearly defined segments, each with a separate set of needs, are best suited to differentiated marketing.

Concentrated marketing: Marketers can use the focused strategy to focus on a particular market segment and use a single marketing mix. With this level of specialisation, a company is better able to compete against larger rivals because it can focus its resources on a single, clearly defined, and well-understood market. It's possible to get pigeonholed into one product and one market by a concentrated marketing strategy, leaving the company exposed to the effects of shifting market conditions.

Micro marketing

Advertisement efforts are concentrated on a small set of highly-targeted consumers in micromarketing. In micromarketing, companies narrowly define their target audience by a specific characteristic, such as ZIP code or job title, and then tailor their campaigns to that specific segment. Customization and the lack of economies of scale can lead to a higher price tag for this method.

POSITIONING OF SERVICES

The uniqueness of a service's placement in a competitive market is known as service positioning. Serving clients' needs and standing out from the competition in a way that resonates with them are hallmarks of an excellent position.

Positioning based on the characteristics of a product or service. An emphasis is placed on addressing a customer's pain point with your product or service. In the case of toothpaste, for example, you might emphasise benefits like teeth whitening or tartar control in your marketing strategy.

PROCESS OF POSITIONING

Product positioning involves a number of steps including the following:

- Determining levels of positioning

- Identification of key attributes of importance to selected segments
- Location of attributes on a positioning map
- Evaluating positioning options
- Implementing positioning.

Determining levels of positioning

As a first stage in the positioning process, it is necessary to identify which levels – service, product sector, and corporate – will be given explicit focus. The decisions made by some service firms will be illustrated with a few examples. The level or levels of positioning to be accomplished are usually quite clear, but certain organisations have placed differing emphasis on these levels at various points in time.

Identification of once positioning has been established, it's time to focus on the characteristics that matter most in each target market In particular, it is important to think about how purchases are made. When deciding whether or not to purchase a service, different people consider various factors.

3. Location of attributes on positioning map

For each of these variables, statistical processes are available to combine them into aggregate dimensions. The positioning process begins with the selection of the most essential attribute and the location of the various companies' services. Depending on how the data were gathered and the statistical processes employed, these dimensions might go by a variety of names, including principal components, multi-dimensional scales, factors, and so on. These two dimensions generally account for a considerable percentage of the "explanation" of the customer's desire on positioning maps.

Products or services are typically plotted on a two dimensional positioning man such as show in the following figure. The positioning map can be relation to the selected attributes. The analysis can be further developed by drawing separate positioning maps for each market segment. Customers in each market segment may perceive the service and its benefits differently and different map will show these different positions.

EVALUATION POSITIONING OPTIONS

- Strengthening current position against competitors to avoid head-on attack.
- Identifying an unoccupied market position that was not filled by a competitor
- Repositioning the competition.

Once a company had identified where it is positioned at present, it then needs to determine how to enhance or sustain its position relative to its competitors.

Criteria for good positioning

- The positioning should be meaningful.
- The positioning must be believable.
- The positioning must be unique.

Implementing positioning and the marketing mix

How a company and service is positioned needs to be communicated throughout all of its implicit and explicit interactions with customers. This suggests that all elements of the company, its staff, policies and image, need to reflect a similar image which together conveys the desires position to the market place. This means that a company must establish a strategic positioning direction, which is followed through in all of its tactical marketing and sales activities.

A successful positioning strategy should make the service clearly distinguishable by features which are desirable and important to the target customer segment. This means that the positioning strategy should be examined from time to time to ensure that it does not become outdated and that it is still relevant to the target market segment.

The marketing mix is the key to implementing a positioning strategy. The design of the marketing mix to implement the positioning must be based on the key salient attributes relevant to the target segment. These attributes should be identified in the context of analysis of competitors, whose positions should be assessed to discover their vulnerability. All the elements of the marketing mix can be utilized to influence the customer"s perception and hence The marketing mix can be used to develop a coherent totality that creates the positioning in the customer"s mind.

IMPORTANCE OF POSITIONING

Both bringing new brands into the market and repositioning existing brands are part of positioning. Keeping items and services distinct from one another is the focus of this discipline.. Positioning a company's offerings in its core market segments, where it is either objectively or subjectivey superior to the offerings of competitors, is essential for maximising its potential.

In the services sector, positioning is very critical. Increasing competition in each market area has resulted in an ever-increasing number of options for consumers. Advertising messages highlighting various aspects of the services are used to convey these offerings. Positioning is all about promoting the company's best features and how well they meet the needs of the target audience.

Customers may find it more difficult and harder to differentiate between services because of the intangibility and other characteristics that go along with them. Customer perceptions of a company's products and services are improved when the company's positioning is clear and distinct from the competition.

Positioning is a strategic marketing tool which allows managers to determine what their position is now,

Exactly what they want it to be and how they intend to get there. The allows for the identification of market possibilities by analysing positions that rivals' products do not fill. Product development and the redesign of current items are influenced by it. It also allows you to think about what your competitors might do and how they might respond. However, it is equally important to think about notion at the sector and organisational levels. The entire marketing plan is based on positioning, which explains why the target market segment should buy your product or service. It also provides guidance for the development of a marketing mix that is consistent with the positioning of the company.

POSITIONING SERVICES IN COMPETITIVE MARKETS

Providers of services are represented by

a. From the speed at which services are provided to the quality of the interactions between consumers and service staff, service speed is a key consideration.

Convenience means that the service is provided at a convenient place and at a convenient time.

POSTIONING STRATEGY:

For long-term relationships, it is about generating and preserving distinguishing qualities that will be observed and cherished by those customers.

It is necessary to comprehend

a. Customers' preferences b.The characteristics of their competitors' products.

I. The pursuit of competitive analysis is hampered by a lack of focus:

As the service industry's competition heats up, it's more important than ever for businesses to find ways to set their offerings apart from the competitors. It's not a possibility, because a company wants to appeal to as many customers as possible.

I The clients' needs, shopping habits, consumption patterns, and geographic spread are all different.

Vs. Determined: Which are more important?

Determining factors:

Among competing choices, these are the traits that shoppers consider most important when making a purchase decision.

Convenience of departure is an example of this.

Allowance for an early arrival.

Access to frequent flier benefits

Reservations are an example of this.

Accomplishments

Quantifiable price that can be quantified and analysed. the way a brand is positioned distinguishes it from the competition:

Positioning an organisation in a distinct market position is the goal of competitive positioning strategy.

1. A corporation needs to establish a place in the minds of its target clients in order to succeed.
2. The posture should be straightforward and consistent, delivering a single message at a time.
3. To be a leader, a company must be distinct from its competitors.
4. It is impossible for a corporation to be everything to everyone, therefore it must narrow its emphasis.

When positioning a business, the goal should be to deter rather than attract competition.

Comparative positioning of copies and products

Positioning the copy:

A person's impression of reality is more important than the actual facts when it comes to making judgments.

The marketing mix's communication parts are essentially linked to positioning, according to marketers.

promotion of a company's image and goodwill among its target audience through advertising, marketing, and public relations

significant distinction in the customer's view.

positioning of a product

To enhance a product's appeal to a specific set of characteristics.

Reducing the purchase price

It is possible to change the hours and locations where it is offered.

• Productivity, cost, and a wide range of options

The marketing role of positioning:

It's critical because it connects external market and competition research with in-house corporate analysis.

Because services are intangible, having a clear positioning plan is important for getting the attention of potential clients.

The company is forced into a position of strength where it must contend with stronger rivals.

Because there is minimal demand from customers, the company is forced into a position that no one else wants.

Product positioning for the organisation is so vague that no one is certain of its specific skill.

No one knows about the company, thus it doesn't even have a place in the market.

CUSTOMER POSITIONING OF SERVICES

Two principles are involved in the positioning of a service for consumers. As a starting point, it refers to where the company or organisation stands in the minds of potential customers. It doesn't matter where a company thinks it stands in the marketplace. Rather, it's what the customers think that's the most significant consideration. Second, placement is always a function of how well you can outperform your rivals. It is common for customers to contrast one service provider's products with those of competitors in the same industry before making their final decision.

METHODS OF POSITIONING

Services can be categorised into six distinct categories. Service qualities, use of application, price/quality relationship, service class user, or rival can all be used to place them in the market.

The qualities of a service are what the service is excellent at. For example, the Federal Government

As the greatest "package delivery" company, Express aims to be the best option for customers.

Positioning can be achieved with the use of an application. It's common for gyms to be situated this way. Some gyms specialise on helping people lose weight, while others focus on exercise and weightlifting or conditioning for those who wish to become in shape. For each role, there is a distinct set of equipment and facility design requirements.

Firms can also exploit the Price-Quality relation to position themselves.

Consumers might also be targeted based on the type of service they receive. Pizza Hut wants to be known as a place where you can get a great pizza at a reasonable price.

A quick food restaurant or diner. In the pizza sector, their "advertisement-in" restaurant".

Some services are ranked based on who is using them. In addition, service providers have the option of positioning themselves in comparison to a rival.

6 Steps to Developing a Successful Positioning Technique

Get a sense of where you are now located.

Does your product or service stand out from the rest of the competition, or are you marketing it like any other item on the market?

You can use your current position in the market to help you plan your next move. If you're going to dig deeper into your competition, you'll need to know where you stand now.

In order to determine your current market position, consider the following:

- What is your company's identity?
- Who are the people you want to reach?

- What is the purpose of your work?
- When compared to your competition, what distinguishes you?
- What are your clients' most pressing concerns?

It's important to remember that we're all drawn to companies that have a distinct voice and personality. Instead of creating a jargon no one can comprehend, talk like a normal person. Start by figuring out who your current and ideal customers are, and then speak to them in their language.

Step 2: Examine your rivals' strategies

After gaining an awareness of your own strengths and weaknesses, it's critical to conduct competitive analysis. Why?

Because conducting competitor research necessitates knowing your competition. You'll be able to see where your weaknesses lie and how you may strengthen them.

There are various ways to find out who your rival is, such as using the following:

Market research should be done. Find out which businesses are listed by performing a quick search with relevant keywords. You can also ask your sales team what potential competitors they come across during the sales process. '

• Listen to your customers. Have a discussion with your customers about the companies and goods they consider prior to making a purchase from your company.

Make the most of social media to your benefit. Users can ask inquiries about products and services on a plethora of free sites. These communities and forums are a great place to find potential competitors in your field.

Once you've figured out who your competitors are, it's time to conduct extensive competitor research. In the end, you want to observe how your competitors have positioned their own brand against yours. So, here are some things you should include in your research:

Competitors' products and services

- The advantages and disadvantages of each
- Successful marketing methods that they employ

This company's place in the market

Step 3: Create a position that is uniquely yours

The key to establishing yourself as an industry leader is figuring out what sets your company apart from the competition and how it can benefit your bottom line.

You're likely to notice something after completing competition research. Some companies have similar strengths and weaknesses, as you may have guessed. If you contrast your offering with theirs, you may discover that one of their flaws is also one of your strengths.

This is what makes your stance distinct, and it's the ideal place to begin building your brand's reputation in the marketplace. Take note of what makes you different from the competition while comparing and analysing your strengths and weaknesses.

Create a mission statement in the fourth step.

This one- or two-sentence statement tells your customers what makes your brand different from the ones of your primary competitors.

Before drafting your positioning statement, consider the following questions from the perspective of industry experts:

- Who is your intended audience?
- What is the category of your product or service?
- What is the most valuable feature of your offering?

Exactly how do you back up that benefit?

In the words of Amazon's positioning statement: "Our vision is to be the earth's most customer-centric company; to provide a place where people can come and find and discover everything they would want to buy online."

Amazon's greatest advantage is that they sell a wide choice of products for everyone, despite the fact that their selection is quite broad. What about the evidence itself? Everything is done through the internet.

Step 5: Come up with a catchy tagline.

You can use a tagline, or better known as a slogan, to communicate with potential customers once you've developed a solid positioning statement. In its place, a concise and simplified version of what you want your clients to know replaces the positioning statement.

Here are a few well-known examples as examples:

L'Oreal: "Because you're worth it."

Nike's motto is "Just do it. "•

"Expect more," says the target. It's cheaper."

You can do it, Home Depot. The answer is yes.

Airline with no frills and low fares for short-haul flights: Southwest Airlines.

You may easily use it in other marketing initiatives to convey your business's message, far more successfully than a lengthy and thorough positioning statement would have.

As a last step, test your marketing strategy.

You can't afford to leave anything to chance, not even your positioning statement. Once you've built your placement, you should test it out and experiment with it to see if it's effective before releasing it to the public.

When conducting testing, it's important to incorporate both quantitative and qualitative methods. The results of these tests will allow you to finalise your marketing positioning and, if necessary, make adjustments to your marketing activities.

DEVELOPING AND MAINTAINING DEMAND AND CAPACITY

In most cases, capacity is managed by trying to balance capacity levels with expected demand. Scheduling personnel, hiring part-time employees, training staff to undertake more than one function, and relying on consumer engagement are some of the solutions available to achieve this goal

Managing a company's capacity is making certain that it is operating at full capacity at all times and in all circumstances. Unfulfilled orders and customer attrition could lead to lower revenues for companies that don't properly manage their capacity.

Strategies for matching capacity and demand

Having a firm grip on the restrictions imposed by its own capacity and the trends in customer demand. In terms of supply and demand, it's in a strong position to come up with ideas.

Demand and capacity shifts

An organization's goal is to move customers away from times when demand exceeds capacity by shifting demand and capacity. Possibly by persuading them to make use of the service while demand is low.

During busy hours, reduce demand.

A service provider's capacity and demand can be aligned by reducing demand during peak periods of demand for service.

Maintain a balance between supply and demand

Service providers may also look at raising demand for service during periods when the service is less than full capacity in order to better balance capacity and demand.

Capacity adjustment in order to satisfy.

MODULE – 5

CHALLENGES OF SERVICE MARKETING

Setting and achieving marketing goals is the end result of a series of activities known as marketing planning, which are carried out in a systematic order.

When it comes to the Marketing Planning Process, it's all about figuring out how to launch and market a product such that it becomes an immediate best seller. This planning includes all of the tactics and procedures used by management to sell their goods in the market and achieve sales goals within the given time frame.

Planning a company's marketing strategy and techniques is done in a methodical manner using a marketing planning process like this: For example, it is prudent to concentrate on the strategic components of a new practise area. Going to market can be described in this manner.

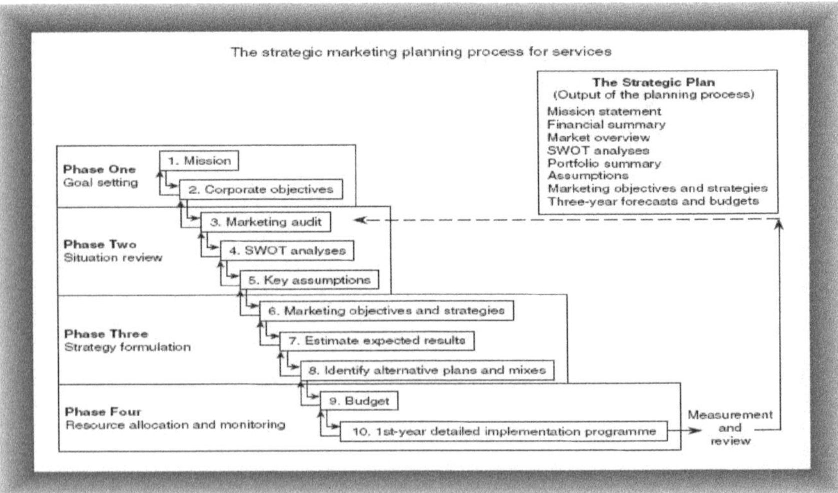

The steps of the planning process are usually similar for every business with minor changes according to the conditions:

1. Developing the action plan

- Setting up the goals and vision
- Setting up the mission statement
- Objectives of the firm

The first and most important step in making a product successful is to carefully observe the goal of the company. It's important to know what you want out of your marketing campaign before you begin preparing. Understanding your ultimate aim is critical, since it reveals your company's mission and goals as well as the direction you want to take the product in.

2. Monitor your current position

- Through marketing audit and monitoring
- SWOT analysis
- The next stage is to take stock of the current state of affairs. It's a subset of a company's long-term and strategic planning processes that shows the company's current status and the resources it has.
- Make a plan for the resources and evaluate them, as well as the elements both inside and outside the organisation. Analyze the potential benefits and drawbacks of releasing the new product. To better infiltrate the market, review the market, select the right one, and divide it into multiple parts using resources.
- Perform a SWOT analysis of the company, which takes into account both internal and external factors. You can use this to assess the existing situation and make adjustments if necessary. Create an internal view of the company that demonstrates that you have a good grasp on the needs of your target audience.
- Investigate the market to learn more about your competition and the changing demands of your target audience, as well as the difficulties associated with meeting those wants.
- In order to take into account some external aspects that are directly linked to the internal capabilities and performance of the

company, you must keep an eye on the current situation while putting the planning process into action. External factors such as the legal system, the political climate, and the level of market competition are all intertwined with internal factors such as the economy, culture, and varied demographics.

3. Developing a strategy for Marketing

- Marketing Mix
- Designing objectives and strategy for marketing
- Vehicles and sources of communication
- Observe the alternative strategies and processes for marketing available
- Marketing strategies and goals are developed in order to achieve the company's overall goal. Marketing methods that are most effective at promoting a firm are observed here. This stage will aid in the selection of various marketing methods that can be used to reach the target market.
- This will assist you in steering you toward the market segment you've chosen to target. What style of marketing and product positioning is most appropriate for a certain market will also be determined by this information.
- As a result, by incorporating the marketing efforts of well-known marketers like Kotler, Porter, and Ansoff, a single market report can be created that details how the product will be introduced, as well as the vehicle they plan to use.
- An effective competitive advantage can be achieved by utilising the marketing mix components in the development of a marketing plan. Incorporating any plan and determining how to implement your marketing efforts in order to target the intended client requires relying on the key strengths of the organisation.

4. Employing, executing and evaluating the planning process

- Make the budget
- Define the resources and implement

- Analyzing and over viewing
- At this point in the planning process, operational level activities are included. A budget for putting into effect the procedures we've spoken about, as well as some specific plans of action, will be outlined in this document. The process must be consistently monitored, and the plan must be observed depending on the customer's opinion and feedback. As a result, the marketing strategy should be reviewed on a frequent basis.

NEED FOR THE PLANNING PROCESS IN MARKETING

According to its original purpose, "to give businesses plans on where they envision their business going in the future," marketing planning was developed. An overview of the target market and its segmentation can be obtained from this document. One of the most critical aspects of this procedure is keeping detailed records of your actions.

If you want your product to succeed on the market, you must carefully develop and implement your marketing techniques. You can't compete in today's market if you don't have a solid plan in place in advance.

Management must devote some time to maximising the company's opportunities by making efficient use of its resources as part of the marketing planning process. The digital marketing trend is currently moving at a rapid rate, thus adequate marketing planning is essential to reach the largest market possible. It's also possible to avoid the danger of failure by implementing a well-thought-out strategy.

DEVELOPING AND MANAGING THE CUSTOMER SERVICE FUNCTION

A company's approach to customer service may be summed up as a procedure that ensures it delivers on its promises time and time again. In order to improve customer service, organisations should break down the service into various service activities, set service standards for each activity, conduct customer surveys on a regular basis, provide the necessary infrastructure and advanced technology and monitor changes in the environment, and introduce changes in the service delivery process.

When it comes to improving customer service, today's businesses are taking full advantage of technology. The customer-service management cycle is a representation of an organization's ongoing efforts to improve customer service. Understanding clients, setting service standards, promoting teamwork and customer orientation, building control mechanisms, and preventing problems rather than fixing them are all part of this cycle.

To enhance the customer's overall experience, many firms offer additional services in addition to their core offering. The service delivery method can also be improved to improve customer service. Organizational performance can be improved by looking at a number of different variables, such as who sells the services, how often customers need to interact with service staff, who hires those services, how long they take to complete, how flexible the provider's capacity is, how frequently those services are bought in, how complex they are and how much risk they involve.

Companies must follow a set of steps in order to implement a successful customer service programme, including hiring the right people for the right jobs, implementing training programmes, answering customers' questions, resolving issues quickly and uniformly, establishing reasonable service prices, outsourcing some activities, attempting to prevent problems, and evaluating employee performance

Using a customer service survey, for example, a brand can determine how satisfied a client was with the service they received from them. In order to retain clients and identify areas of service that need improvement, this survey is essential.

An organization's success depends on its ability to provide excellent customer service. In addition to advertising and branding operations, it's that one entity that supports all other customer engagement efforts. The Net Promoter Score (NPS) is an indicator of a brand's capacity to be recommended and shared by its customers.

Importance of good customer service with examples:

"Customer service shouldn't just be a department, it should be the entire company." – Zappos' founder Tony Hsieh

- Every time a customer comes to us with a problem, they want us to solve it and leave them satisfied. That's the level of customer service an organisation should be able to provide in order to stand the test of time.
- **Accelerated response time**: Almost three-quarters of customers expect a response within five minutes of posting a question online. Because of the rise in the number of companies focusing on customer service, every company is seeking to prioritise the touchpoints that form a full client experience.
- **Efficient management of customer problems:** When it comes to determining a company's long-term success or failure, how it handles customer complaints and provides a better customer experience is critical.
- **Offer adequate customer service**: To be successful, a business needs to provide high-quality products and services as well as excellent customer service. Customer experience can be enhanced by interacting with the target audience on a variety of levels.
- Each customer service counts: Reduced sales are a direct result of providing subpar products and services, and unhappy consumers are likely to tell their friends and colleagues about their unpleasant experience, which can hurt a company's reputation in the marketplace. Focus on making the customer's experience enjoyable if they encounter a problem with a product so that they will continue to support the company.

Why is a happy customer a source for better business?

- People naturally demand the best possible service or product from your company. They also demand the best customer service in the event of questions or assistance. It's one of the main reasons they stay with a company for so long. More satisfied customers are more inclined to stay loyal to your brand.
- **Make the best use of word of mouth**: An effective marketing strategy relies on the power of word-of-mouth. Customers who have had a positive experience are more likely to spread the word about the company's products and services, which can lead to an increase in sales. The Net Promoter Score (NPS) can be calculated by incorporating the NPS question into a customer satisfaction survey.
- **Implement developed technology**: Improved or maintained customer service is now easier to achieve because to technological improvements. Email, chat, online surveys, social networking sites, and the telephone are all utilised to give ongoing customer service before, during, and after a purchase.
- **Consider time as a key factor:** Maintaining good relations with clients is critical to their success. In order to provide excellent customer service, it is important to provide prompt solutions to customers' issues and to recognise that their time is valuable.
- For example, every time we go out to eat, we have to have a conversation about what to order. How satisfied were you with the service you received? Whether or whether the management was paying attention to the specifications or if the clients were provided cold water when they requested warm water? A vastly improved customer experience can be achieved by having excellent customer service abilities.

TYPES OF CUSTOMER SERVICE:

When working with a consumer, it is critical to know what they want and need. The reputation of a company is based on the quality of its customer service. Some of the most successful customer-focused businesses regularly perform customer service surveys with their target audience utilising powerful customer survey software. In order to become more customer-oriented, a firm can use sophisticated analytics software to do extensive research.

Different customers expect different types of assistance from an organization. There are 5 main types of customer services:

- **Assistance for potential customers:**
- When a potential customer shows interest in a product or service by giving contact information on a company website, contacting the sales support team via online chat, or meeting with a representative offline, that person is considered a "potential customer," not a "current customer." The initial layer of a sales funnel is comprised of these potential clients, who will need ongoing guidance in order to become consumers.
- These potential customers need to know exactly what to expect from the products and services before they buy them, and the customer service staff is responsible for providing that information. For the products they're interested in, continually share resources like product page links and assistance files with them. Insist on them knowing that you have a group of people ready to assist them at all times.
- **Onboarding new customers:** In this category are customers who have already purchased a product or service, but still need assistance in understanding how it works. That's when a customer care team comes into play, to supply all the additional information feasible. Even after a consumer has made a purchase, delivering fast customer service and assistance will help turn them into repeat customers over time.

- By spending time with a new customer, customer service teams tend to build stronger relationships with the majority of their customers..
- **Guidance to impulsive customers:** They will buy in a flash if everything about the goods and services is well-explained and they are certain of what they need. In order to persuade customers to buy, the process of purchasing things must be simple and quick. When making an online purchase, it's best to provide as much detail and make as few clicks as possible.
- Customers who are prone to acting on the spur of the moment need a quick fix. These impulsive customers may leave the website session if the answer takes too long.
- **Assist customers looking for discounts:** These customers will never buy from an organisation at the stated price. At every given price point, consumers will look for something extra in a product or service. They may not buy the same things again, if they cannot get a discount, if they have previously purchased them at a lower price.
- Products must be constantly improved so that buyers will agree to purchase them. Assist in whatever way you can, whether it's via promo codes or something else! For every setback these clients encounter, customer service might encourage them to stay longer with a firm.
- **Support the loyalists:** Customers like this can be relied upon to spread the word about your business. They'll make sure they buy from the same company and contribute significantly to the business. They'll tell their friends and relatives about your goods and services, which will result in more sales for you. Talk to your most loyal customers on a regular basis to learn what they think of your products and services and why they remain loyal to your company.
- More than just providing assistance, a customer service team's primary duty is to ensure the long-term success of the company by actively engaging with customers/clients. Use social media or a website to disseminate a case study based on

their experience. Make an effort to implement the procedures outlined below in order to transform these clients into repeat buyers of your products.

Tips to improve customer service skills:

Customer service relies heavily on the contributions of employees. Customer-facing teams, such as customer service or sales teams, should receive frequent training to improve their customer satisfaction skills.. It is important to keep an eye on things like their ability to communicate, principles at work, experience in the subject matter, and ability to solve problems.

In order to keep everyone happy, it is important to keep everyone involved.

"Investors want a return on their money. People are more likely to pitch in when they have a stake in the project. It's Simon Sinek. Employees are less likely to perform to the best of their ability unless and until they feel valued, respected, and regularly engaged in their work. Employee dissatisfaction surveys can be used by management to get information from disgruntled workers who may not be able to publicly express their disapproval. When employees are able to remain anonymous in this way, they are able to give honest and clear feedback.

Every interaction with a company's customers should be a positive one. Determine which aspects of customer service are operating well and which ones require improvement from every angle. A manager's job will be easier if he or she can focus on the positive aspects of the business and ensure that consumers are satisfied at every touchpoint.

An effective relationship with consumers relies on great customer service abilities within the company. In order to find a common interest with customers, the representatives can be trained to ask the right questions or to understand customer problems actively and solve them in real time, or to follow up with clients even after their problems have been resolved. In addition, this can aid in the development of new products and services.

Send customer satisfaction surveys to a specific group of customers so that they can tell others about their experiences with the company. A consumer's feedback from these surveys can be utilised to plan for a better customer experience the next time they shop with an organisation.

DEVELOPING AND MAINTAINING QUALITY OF SERVICES

The customer's evaluation of a company's performance in relation to their service expectations is referred to as service quality. High-quality service providers are likely to be able to meet the needs of their customers while maintaining a competitive edge in their market.

In the service industry, a willingness to deliver high-quality service is critical. Because of the importance of providing high-quality services to these companies' survival and success, as well as the fact that doing so is a viable business strategy.

Regularly assess the effectiveness of your company's customer service activities. Make improvements to client service. Organize a reward system for employees that go above and beyond in their customer service efforts. On a frequent basis, review your customer service strategy.

As an illustration, consider being courteous and respectful to a customer. Being able to connect with others. Being a good listener is an example of how to be a decent person. Physical facilities and enabling products are tangibles.

Once service providers have reached their targeted level of quality, they face the next great challenge: maintaining that level of perfection. Establishing and maintaining service standards is just as crucial as doing so in the first place.

A proactive or a reactive approach can be taken by any company to ensure that service standards are met.Proactive: A proactive approach entails actively reaching out to customers and trying to gather their feedback on service quality and suggested areas of improvement. This can be done by way of

- Surveys and administering questionnaires

- Gap Analysis, and
- Staff training

a. **Surveys and questionnaires**: Such an approach helps a brand to anticipate customer demands and expectations and align its service offering accordingly. Also, the findings of such surveys can help to identify common issues and demands of customers hence helping a company to customize its service offering.

b. **Gap Analysis:** Another approach that is adopted for analyzing service quality is that of the gap analysis. The company has an ideal service standard that it would like to offer to its customers. This is contrasted with the current level of service being offered. The gap thus identified serves both as a measure and as a basis for planning a future course of action to improve the service offering.

c. **Staff Training:** Another crucial aspect of the proactive approach is staff training. Companies nowadays spend generously on training their personnel to adequately handle customer queries and/or complaints. This is particularly true if a company is changing its service offering or going in for a price hike of its existing services. For example, when a fast food chain increases the price of its existing products, the staff has to handle multiple customer queries regarding the hike. Lack of a satisfactory explanation would signify poor service standards and lead to customer dissatisfaction.

Reactive: When a consumer complains about poor service quality, a reactive strategy involves using a specified service recovery process. Apologizing to the customer is usually the first step, followed by taking actions to rectify the situation. This strategy has a fundamental flaw: the customer has already had a bad experience with the brand's service in this instance.

MEASURING SERVICE QUALITY

In order to ensure that service quality is maintained, it is important to have a method of "measuring" quality in place. A company's nature, service model, and client expectations will all influence the parameters that are chosen. An example of a measure for assessing the quality of customer service would be the average time it takes to handle a call or resolve a complaint at a telecom provider's call centre. Customer footfall or sales growth month over month can be used to gauge the level of customer service provided by a fast food restaurant's employees.

In order to enforce the service level the company seeks to maintain, a quality measurement system must first be put in place.

WAYS TO MAINTAIN QUALITY OF SERVICES

1. Evaluate and analyze customer interactions

Every call to a call centre is recorded as regular procedure. It's the method by which contact centres assess and evaluate client encounters that separates the effective ones from the average ones.

Managers of call centres can learn a lot about their agents' strengths and limitations by doing quality monitoring.

It is possible to monitor and analyse patterns in customer interactions through the use of call recordings.

2. Provide continuous coaching

After onboarding, agent training should continue indefinitely. You may boost customer service operations in general by providing agents with continual training and mentoring.

Constant coaching is a terrific approach to build up your firm's knowledge capital and ensure that your company can grow a wide range of expertise over time.

To ensure that your company's bottom line benefits, you should hire only the most qualified individuals.

3. Evaluate the effectiveness of KPI's regularly

Using key performance indicators (KPIs), call centres may determine how well their customer support operations are working.

However, relying too much on KPI's might stifle a company's growth or divert attention from the genuine actions and procedures that can improve customer experience.

The call center's KPI's should be evaluated by managers to verify that agents are focusing their efforts on customer satisfaction.

4. Monitor all feedback channels

For a call centre, customer feedback is an invaluable resource for enhancing service standards.

Long-term business success is heavily influenced by how well organisations utilise customer feedback. Why? Customer satisfaction is a dependable indicator of a company's ability to succeed.

In order to improve the quality of your customer service in the future, you must maintain track of and evaluate consumer feedback channels such post-call surveys, feedback request emails, social media, and online reviews.

5. Stay on top of the latest technology trends

Companies, including call centres, need to stay on top of the latest developments in technology in order to remain competitive.

Using the most up-to-date call centre software is just the beginning. You need to keep up with the current technology advancements in order to come up with efficient company plans.

It's always a good idea to stay up to date on the latest technical developments, as they can open up new business opportunities that your competitors may not even be aware of.

5 WAYS TO MAINTAIN THE QUALITY OF YOUR CUSTOMER SERVICE

Maintaining and Improving the Service Personnel Quality and Performance!

These suggestions are merely meant to give you an idea of the types of actions that a service firm might do. Many behaviours and activities fall into more than one category, and a variety of different options may be evaluated.

A. Careful Selection and Training of Service Personnel:

Because many services require personal touch, recruiting, selection and training and development programmes must be tailored to the demands of the services being given. Employees need to know exactly what they're doing. This necessitates the creation of comprehensive job descriptions. It's also important to establish the qualities that are required of those who work in customer service positions.

It is customary to classify service occupations based on factors such as educational requirements, prior work history, interpersonal abilities, and more. One current idea is that service sector workers should be separated into groups based on the communication expectations of their consumers. A company's communication style may be a key factor in determining desired employee traits. Attention must be paid to how the project will be managed and arranged.

B. Internal Marketing:

Reiterating the importance of marketing to those who service external clients is the goal of internal marketing idea. When it comes to internal marketing, that means using the same philosophy that benefits the company's external clients to hire and retain the best employees and motivate them to do their best work.

The Internal Marketing Concept

As a result of this interpretation, employees are considered as internal customers and their jobs as internal products that must be tailored to better fulfil the needs of consumers. To be a more effective service company, an organisation must provide its employees with better and more pleasant work opportunities. Internal marketing is of crucial importance since staff may be reluctant to sell a service product which they do not find acceptable. This point can be illustrated by the attitude of some staff to the banks' new charging policies for credits collected for other banks.

During the introduction of these policies, some staff would not accept the directive to charge customers for using the service partly due to certain long-established customer relationships. The policy had to be modified and ended in an authority to charge only when 'feasible'.

C. Using Practices to Other Consistent Behaviour:

Consistent behaviour among employees is another challenge for the service business. As a result of the consumer's actions, the company's human representatives will act in a different way, and the quality of service they provide will be affected. A bank's branches may offer the same services to its customers, but individual cashiers' ability to 'produce' these services varies greatly.

Many non-profits strive to maintain a consistent level of human effort. Service businesses must clearly specify protocols for some of their services in order to ensure that they are consistently performed.

Such a method has the potential to become excessively mechanical. In most organisations, there is a delicate balancing act to be struck between too much rigidity and too little. Customers' wide range of preferences necessitates procedures that can accommodate the inherent uncertainty. The following is an outline of a recent initiative by a Service Company to improve customer service, including the training of current employees.

Customer Services Campaign Plan:

1. Communication with Management and Staff:

Efforts at the greatest level of competency necessitate a high level of employee involvement in the company's goals. To do this, it is vital to design and implement a professional strategy to staff communication. It's necessary to conduct a thorough analysis on the best medium for this task.

2. Training:

An essential part of customer service training is making sure no random selections are made.

Identifying the units where customer service training is relevant and taking the necessary steps to schedule courses and personnel lists is therefore crucial. It should also be made plain to employees who have been nominated that the purpose of any training programme is to improve customer service standards.

3. Management / Staff Relationships

In addition to involving employees in business policies, another aspect is to give them a sense of belonging and demonstrate that the organisation cares about their difficulties. To do this, managers and supervisors must go to the "shop floor," where the workers are.

4. Customer Service Improvement:

This campaign is all about creating changes and improvements. Either a new technique or service can be introduced, or an employee's attitude can be changed. As a result, we need to be aware of and prepared to address many of the challenges that our consumers face.

5. Link Major Changes to Customer Service

It will be difficult to get commitment to a customer service campaign if staff does not see evidence of effort to remove some of the production inadequacies which frustrate them. There must be, there-fore, a means of passing on to all personnel, information on the effects that a change has been made, however small.

Rewards for Outstanding Individual Performance

Whether it's a simple "well done" or an unique Customer Service Awards Scheme, this should be a big part of the campaign. As a result, we must establish a policy among all section heads to recognise individual performance. Consider the possibility of a reward programme, perhaps in the form of complimentary tickets, with a committee in place to review suggestions.

Ensuring Consistent Appearance:

A service organization's physical appearance and its staff are typically its only tangible elements, due to the intangibility of many services. Consumers can be expected to choose a service provider that clearly indicates the grade of service desired for the fulfilment of their needs through their location and sales staff. The appearance of service people is one of the ways in which corporations strive to project an image and convey a sense of quality.

Service management can influence the appearance of service people. The adoption of 'uniforms' and types of dress can help achieve this goal. Hotel waiters, airline stewardesses, and mechanics at a car service centre may all be obliged to dress in a certain way. Formality might range from a top coat to a full uniform, with all of the necessary accessories.

Further standardization of appearance may be accomplished by recruiting service personnel with specific characteristics (e.g. of a certain height or age range). Also the service organization may provide facilities to encourage personal care like hairdressing and beauty parlours. Even when a service organization does not require the wearing of a formal uniform for protective or promotional purposes, an 'acceptable' style of dress may be deliberately encouraged (e.g. amongst bankers and stockbrokers).

Equally 'unacceptable' dress styles may be discouraged. Such uniforms help create standards of 'uniformity' and thus are an important input to the overall image of a service organization, where uniformity is required. Where uniformity is not required, service organizations may encourage varying styles of non-conforming dress to cultivate an unconventional image of variety (e.g. as in advertising agencies).

MODULE – 6

RELATIONSHIP MARKETING

Relationship marketing is a aspect of consumer dating management (CRM) that focuses on purchaser loyalty and long-term consumer engagement in place of shorter-term dreams like purchaser acquisition and man or woman sales. The goal of relationship advertising (or client relationship marketing) is to create robust, even emotional, client connections to a logo which can cause ongoing commercial enterprise, loose word-of-mouth promoting and data from clients that can generate leads.

Relationship advertising refers to advertising efforts that makes a specialty of developing long-term dating with clients. It is part of Customer dating management (CRM) which pursuits to acquire lengthy-term engagement of clients with enterprise for maintaining its profitability. Relationship advertising and marketing is distinct from other forms of traditional advertising and marketing.

It carries out sports for achievement of lengthy-term goals like client loyalty. Whereas, traditional advertising works closer to getting quick-term desires like consumer acquisition and one-time income. Traditional advertising and marketing does now not pay any attention on constructing relationships. Relationship advertising and marketing as opposed to sales transactions emphasizes on client retention and their pleasure degree.

Companies find it value-effective in advertising their products to existing clients as they don't want to run mass promotional campaigns. Nowadays, brands run customized marketing campaigns for communicating with audience that enables them in knowledge consumer desires correctly. Long term clients also are less in all likelihood to churn which broaden close relationships with emblem thereby generating extra income for them.

Relationship advertising and marketing stands in evaluation to the more traditional transactional advertising approach, which makes a specialty of increasing the range of person sales. In the transactional model, the return on client acquisition fee may be inadequate. A customer may be convinced to pick that logo one time, however without a robust dating advertising and marketing approach, the customer might not come again to that brand within the destiny. While organizations integrate factors of each dating and transactional advertising, consumer courting advertising and marketing is starting to play a more critical function for many groups.

Relationship Marketing is a approach of Customer Relationship Management (CRM) that emphasizes customer retention, pride, and lifelong purchaser cost. Its motive is to marketplace to current customers as opposed to new client acquisition thru sales and advertising.

A correct courting advertising strategy is rooted in constructing consumer loyalty and lasting, long-time period engagement along with your patron base. Benefits encompass expanded wonderful phrase-of-mouth, repeat business, and a willingness at the patron's element to provide precious remarks to the organisation and their friends.

Relationship Marketing is a contemporary approach to advertising and marketing which specializes in improving the purchaser revel in and developing purchaser loyalty as opposed to growing the sales quantity and income of the enterprise. Keeping the clients engaged and presenting them with the best feasible price from their purchase is important. Here comes the position of dating marketing.

When the competition is excessive, and the clients are aware, the organizations can't just depend upon selling their services or products to them.

The customers constantly search for the groups which give an delivered price or advantage to them alongside the service or product.

For Example; Nike, being the most recognized athletic wear brands, started its 'Just Do it' campaign to capture the attention of the non-athletes.

The advertisement featured a heavy boy wearing Nike apparel and running. Thus, it recognized the overweight people and tried to motivate them through the message that everything is possible if we try to do it.

IMPORTANCE OF RELATIONSHIP MARKETING

Acquiring new clients can be hard and luxurious. Relationship advertising and marketing facilitates keep customers over the long time, which leads to purchaser loyalty rather than clients buy as soon as or once in a while.

Relationship advertising and marketing is important for its capability to stay in near contact with customers. By know-how how clients use a logo's services and products and watching additional unmet desires, manufacturers can create new capabilities and offerings to satisfy those desires, in addition strengthening the relationship.

- **Increase in Sales Volume**: Enhanced client enjoy method an clean up promoting and pass-promoting of products or offerings to happy customers. This ultimately increases sales quantity.
- **Low Advertisement Cost:** successful dating advertising and marketing reduces the efforts on client acquisition because it helps in preserving clients for lengthy-time period. Thus, decreasing the commercial value.
- **High-Profit Better Price**: A glad customer tends to good buy less for the fees and is prepared to pay a truthful rate for the products or services. This increases the earnings margin of the seller.
- **Creates Brand Image**: A satisfied consumer will sell the services or products amongst their peers, household and the acknowledged ones. This word of mouth creates a robust logo picture of the organization.

- **Customer Retention**: Customer acquisition isn't everything; meeting the customer needs, creating fee for the clients and making them purchase time and again is crucial. All that is viable thru consumer dating advertising.
- **Gain a cutthroat frame:** A unswerving consumer feels comfortable shopping for items or services from one single shop in place of shopping around at various locations. This is a bonus for the company over its competitors.

STRATEGIES OF RELATIONSHIP MARKETING

Based on customer experience control (CEM), relationship marketing focuses on improving customer interactions in order to build stronger brand loyalty. Despite the fact that these interactions might still take place in person or over the phone, a large portion of dating advertising and CEM has moved to the Internet.

Because of the volume of data available online and the growing popularity of social media, most buyers expect to be able to quickly find out specifics about a brand and even expect to be able to persuade products and services by posting about them on social media or reading online reviews. Today's dating advertising and marketing involves fostering cordial relations between the company and its customers, keeping tabs on their hobbies and interests, and delivering relevant information to them based on that information.

With the use of an individual profile on an e-commerce website, for instance, the website might preserve the user's data for future visits and provide them more personalised content material the subsequent time they visit the site. Allowing visitors to check in via Facebook or any other social media channel allows them to have an easier customer experience and connects them to your brand's social media accounts.

Customer relationship management (CRM) and advertising and marketing automation (A/M) software can help with this by making it easier to store, organise, and use customer records. When used in conjunction with dating advertising and marketing in social media, social CRM tools may help businesses better communicate with their customers and maintain a positive brand image by allowing them to more easily post and respond to customer issues on social media platforms.

In today's virtual world, it is more of a need than a choice to maintain long-term relationships with customers. This is because customers are free to express their thoughts about their shopping experiences via social media.

It's up to the employer to decide whether or not to generate value for the current customers or lose the potential customers as well.

Know Your Customer: KYC is all about retaining song of the vital records about the clients and their necessities. It helps in supplying a better provider to the clients and attaining out to a more specific audience.

Customer Service: Customer service and support should be a top priority for every firm that sells products or services to customers. Consumers, management, and employees should all be aware of the importance of a company's commitment to its customers.

Email Marketing: In order to keep up with previous and current customers, you can use email marketing. The best way to do this is to teach children about the ins and outs of giving and selling, and to wish them well on special occasions like holidays and fairs. Gives them a sense of worth.

Customer Awareness and Education: One of the finest techniques to dating advertising is to educate and train clients instead of trying to advertise the products or services and the benefits they bring.

Customer Feedback: The high-quality manner to reveal the clients that their idea and experience topics to the organization are to take the feedback from them. It also enables in enhancing the product or service as consistent with the consumer need.

SMS Marketing: Mobile phones have been the most popular method of successful communication in recent years.

Organizations can keep in touch with their customers by sending them messages to help, address queries, take feedback, and so on.

Online Marketing: Online marketing has developed as a revolution in recent years as a way for businesses to promote, gather, and maintain a large customer base. Most popular online shopping platforms include eBay and Amazon as well as Alibaba.

Social Media: Today, the majority of people's time is spent on social networking websites like Facebook, Twitter, Instagram, and so on. As a means of attracting and retaining consumers, firms use these frameworks to gather information about their needs, preferences, and concerns, among other things.

Loyalty/Referral Program: The most prevalent kind of relationship management is running loyalty programmes or referral programmes. It is rewarding customers with points each time they make a purchase from a specific save, which they can redeem for a variety of benefits, such as freebies or discounts.

The referral software is some other way wherein the prevailing customers are rewarded for growing more clients for the commercial enterprise via mouth publicity.

ERP and CRM Technology: Companies utilise Customer Relationship Management (CRM) to maintain track of their current and potential customers. This allows them to share their thoughts on the products and services they've purchased..

In order to improve the client experience, the agency uses Enterprise Resource Planning (ERP) software, which makes it easy for CRM data to be shared between departments.

Questionnaires and Surveys are two terms that describe the same thing. Having a questionnaire filled out by former customers might help a company better understand the market difficulties they encounter before or after making a purchase.

In this way, the company can discover the reasons why customers have shifted to a new product or service or another company.

BENEFITS OF RELATIONSHIP MARKETING

Benefits of courting marketing consist of:

Patrons who pay a higher lifetime charge (CLV). Relationship marketing produces loyal customers, which leads to repeat purchases and a greater CLV. In addition, loyal customers are more likely to become brand champions or ambassadors, promoting the company's products and services to their friends, family, and professional contacts.

Reduction in the amount spent on advertising and other forms of promotion. Advertising and marketing expenses to bring in new clients might be expensive. Relationship advertising, often known as "buzz marketing," gets customers to spread the word about a company on their own. Customers' word-of-mouth advertising for a brand's goods and services can result in increased sales. High-quality dating advertising bundles necessitate no advertising or marketing expenditures from the brands.

Organizational alignment around the consumer should be strengthened. Relationship-based businesses have a deeper organisational alignment around delivering a great customer experience. The teams work together to ensure that customers are happy and satisfied in the long run.

Examples of relationship marketing

To facilitate dating advertising, a variety of sports brands might be utilised. These include:

Customers who are consistently impressed by the quality of a company's customer care are far more inclined to stick with the brand.

- **Send a social media post or a wonder gift card to customers as a way of saying thanks.**
- Soliciting customer feedback via surveys, polls, and phone calls can have a significant impact on the perception that customer feedback is respected and contributes to the development of better products and services.
- Create a customer loyalty programme that rewards customers

for their long-term business.

- Establish a network of customers by hosting events for your customers.

  Encourage word-of-mouth advertising and marketing by creating customer advocacy or logo advocacy packages.
- Offer discounts or perks to long-term or repeat customers

LEVELS OF CUSTOMER RELATIONSHIPS

A customer's journey can be broken down into three stages, each representing a different level of relationship marketing.

- **Level 1: Customer-specific customization....**
- **Rewarding client loyalty at the Level 2 level.**

Reaching out to high-value clients on a more intimate level at Level 3.

The Loyal Customer: When it comes to customer connections, this is the ultimate goal. They buy from you when they do so. It's no longer effective for competitors to call; they no longer accept offers or appointments. As a result of your connections at every level of the company, you are able to retain a firm grasp on profit margins. In addition, loyal customers spread the word about your business whenever they hear of someone who could benefit from your products or services. For any customer who is not this degree, you should have a strategy in place before transporting them on this route.

The Habitual Buyer: Habitual Buyers may appear to be Loyal Customers, but this isn't always the case. You're their go-to vendor whenever they make a buy. A Habitual Buyer, on the other hand – and this is a critical distinction – gives you very little wiggle room. If you make a mistake with a delivery (and let's be honest, we all make mistakes occasionally), you risk losing their business. Reopen the shopping options by charging a price. When working with Habitual Buyers, you may find that they are more careful about who they interact with and how they deal with you. While Habitual

Buyers can be fooled into thinking they're Loyal Customers, a competitor can appear out of nowhere and steal from them.

The Occasional Buyer – Simply put, the Occasional Purchaser is just that. For the most part, Occasional Buyers have no clear pattern to their purchases (unless, of course, if you're losing business on price). When it comes to the occasional buyer, you and your rivals are just somewhere to shop for goods. Shopping agents tend to deal only with Occasional Buyers, which is as true an argument as any in opposition to dealing solely with shopping agents.

"Dating shop clerk" can have more loyal customers than other salespeople, and they'll have a game plan in place for progressing Habituals to Loyals and Ocassionally-to-Habitual customers. In order to get there, you have to put in lots of hard work and study while also focusing on the marketing strategy. An uncomfortable level of honesty is also included. It's difficult to detect the many clients who aren't Loyal Customers among ego-driven salespeople (which can include the majority of individuals). However, if you're looking for a great approach to grow your business in 2015, you should identify all of your most important customers by the three degrees above, and then devise a game plan to move them up. Your boss, as well as your bank account, will be grateful.

DEMENSION OF RELATIONSHIP MARKETING

Trust:

Trust can be described as "a willingness to rely on an trade associate in whom one has self belief." (Moorman et al., 1993) It has been considered as one of the essential factors for a long-lasting courting. Trust could reinforce a long time dating.

Bonding

Adewusi (2008) states in his take a look at that better the extent of bonding with the company, greater they tend to be dependable to such corporations however absence of bond has a poor effect on client dating consequences.

Competence

Selner (1998) states that competence is "the consumer's notion of the provider's technological and business competence". Once clients understand the employer to be equipped they are more likely to stay with them and for this reason can be used as a Relationship Marketing construct to look at its effect on client loyalty.

Commitment

According to Ndubisi (2006), dedication is a important expectation or norm inside business relationships, even as Lacey and Morgan (2007) determined that dedication is nicely ingrained in the connection literature and critical to the creation and protection of advertising relationships. Liang and Wang (2006) confirmed that dedication has an critical position in dating and located that dedication is excellent when the relationships on each sides flip to be extra stable.

Communication

Communication became formulated by Anderson and Narus (1990) as the exchange of timely information among companies. The clients have a variety of assets to acquire the communications such as focused magazines, on line assets, coupons and so forth. Apart from this in addition they benefit statistics from assets such as services capes, customer service departments and provider come across interactions with employees. Hence this paves way to establish dating with clients.

Conflict managing

The typical level of war of words in the running partnership (Anderson and Narus 1990).Conflict displays the disappointment between a consumer and a dealer. Conflict managing is an possibility Journal of Advance Research in Business, Management for the enterprise to reveal its purchaser its efforts to clear up the conflict with an outcome of loyalty if it's miles carried out effectively

Empathy

Seeking to understand the goals and desires of someone else. (Sin et al2005). It is defined as looking for to recognize somebody elses'goals and dreams. In the service marketing literature empathy is used in growing the SERVQUAL test tool for provider best

Reciprocity

"The element of a commercial enterprise dating that reasons either birthday party to offer favours or make allowances for the other in return for similar favours or allowances at a later degree"(Sin et al2005)

Relationship blessings

"Partners that supply superior benefits will be distinctly valued and corporations will devote themselves to setting up, developing and keeping relationships with such partners" Morgan & Hunt (1994). For a lengthy time period dating to exist, both the provider provider and the consumer ought to benefit from this type of dating. Such advantages would set off the service providers to provide better services andalusite customer to be dependable to the organisation.

Shared values

The volume to which partners have beliefs in commonplace about what behaviours, dreams and rules are essential, unimportant, suitable or beside the point, and proper or wrong Morgan & Hunt (1994)

Service Quality

Parasuraman et al (1988) described service pleasant as the consumers' judgement about a firm's typical excellence or superiority. Delivering superior best to the clients is important to the formation of patron loyalty (Zeithaml et al., 1996). Hence the competitive advantage of a service enterprise is determined by way of its capability to amplify and maintain alarge and loyal purchaser base

Technology

Research indicates that successfully handling customers relies upon at the firm's potential to address the changes because of the implementation of Information Technology and its potential to use assets to construct relationships with customers (Payne and Frow, 2005).

Customer Satisfaction

DELIGHT is a "universal rating mostly based on the total buy and consumption experience over the years with a terrific or service," according to Garbarino and Johnson (1999). In Lovelock et al. (1998), the qualities of consumer pride were catalogued (paraphrase).: First and foremost, customer happiness is a direct result of customer loyalty and the willingness of a company to court that loyalty. As a second benefit, satisfied customers share positive word of mouth about a company's service and serve as a marketing tool for the company itself.

Third, fantastically glad customers may be more tolerant as they'd enjoyed an excellent provider delivery in advance.In the literature (Herrmann and Johnson, 1999; Dick and Basu, 1994) it's far emphasised that there may be a substantially wonderful correlation among client delight and Journal of Advance Research in Business, Management and

Customer Loyalty

According to Payne & Richard (1993), "relationship advertising makes a specialty of clients' retention and building long term relations that, in alternate contributes to loyalty. The better the satisfaction perceived by the customer, better the probability for long time family members and increased profitability". Customer loyalty is vital if a enterprise has to retain its current clients. Service services generally keep in mind patron loyalty as an essential source of aggressive advantage(Woodruff, 1997)loyalty will increase repurchase Because loyal clients are more receptive to counter persuasion and unfavorable word of mouth, behaviour. Competition's promotional activities may have less of an impact on loyal customers, who may be less concerned about spending and hence less likely to defect (2003)

GOAL OF RELATIONSHIP MARKETING

It is the goal of courting advertising (also known as "consumer relationship marketing") to build long-lasting, even emotional bonds between a company's logo and its customers so that these relationships can lead to repeat business, free advertising, and customer feedback that can generate new business.

Relationship Marketing is a method of Customer Relationship Management (CRM) that emphasizes client retention, satisfaction, and lifelong client fee. Its cause is to marketplace to modern-day clients as opposed to new purchaser acquisition via income and advertising.

Building robust relationships is the ultimate intention of all associated marketing strategies.

To this end, it objectives to:

Demonstrate your care and concern for clients: With each interplay with customers, companies, shareholders, providers, and your employees, dating advertising techniques intention to expose them which you take care of their welfare. This is executed by way of taking an emotional, empathetic method to the relationship rather than a transactional/sales technique.

Responding as it should be: Relationship advertising and marketing prioritizes consumer interactions. That is why active listening is a cornerstone of this strategy. You can use social media equipment and records to be had via your internet site to facilitate this. As a end result, you are higher capable of reply greater accurately and right away for your customer.

Add value: One of the important factors of a relationship is that it adds value to all of the events worried. As a enterprise owner, you may provide a variety of useful statistics to site visitors to your website. This may be within the shape of brief schooling modules, instructional blogs, enterprise information, opinion portions, comments and reviews with the aid of long-time period customers, product/service tech facts, e-books, whitepapers, and so on.

Profitability: Businesses exist to make profits. Relationship advertising strategies ensure that profitability is boosted because:

- Client acquisition costs are lower
- Loyal customers are much more likely to spend increasingly regularly
- Long-term customers are greater open to new services and innovation
- Your advertising spend is a good deal lower
- Personnel and shareholders are extra linked for your enterprise emotionally, lowering turnover

Collecting Data: Relationship advertising and marketing is one of the smartest methods to gather more in-depth and comprehensive statistics in your customer. Your internet site affords you with sizeable quantities of facts on demographics, conduct, income, buying styles, frequency, comments, and so on. That you can use to your advantage. Usable statistics helps you to customise your services higher and additionally provide applicable and well timed statistics to your customers.

Personalization: An essential purpose of dating advertising is personalization. As a commercial enterprise proprietor, turning in the best, interesting and useful message to the patron on the right time and the right rate factor has been the Holy Grail of advertising for the reason that sunrise of trade. Knowing your customer, and being able to are expecting their future movements, desires, needs and behaviors assist you to streamline your operations and make higher financial projections.

Advocacy: With relationship advertising, your clients grow to be an extension of your marketing branch. Loyal clients tend to come to be marketing evangelists. They make efforts to unfold the phrase to buddies and circle of relatives and involve their social circle of influence in many of their buying decisions. When you deliver steady UX they're higher able to showcase your commercial enterprise, products, and offerings in a higher mild on social media.

REFERENCES:

1. Service Marketing Book by Mary Bitner and Valarie Zeithaml, 1996
2. Service Marketing and Management Book by Audrey Gilmore, 2003
3. Services Marketing Managementbook by Angela Pirrie and Peter Mudie, 2006
4. Handbook Of Services Marketing And Managementoriginally Published: 19 November 1999,Teresa A. Swartz

www.ingramcontent.com/pod-product-compliance
Ingram Content Group UK Ltd.
Pitfield, Milton Keynes, MK11 3LW, UK
UKHW021919190726
13853UKWH00002B/746